TEACHING ABOUT RACE AND RACISM

IN THE COLLEGE CLASSROOM

TEACHING AND LEARNING IN HIGHER EDUCATION
James M. Lang, Series Editor

Other titles in the series:

TEACHING ABOUT RACE AND RACISM
in the **COLLEGE CLASSROOM**

Notes from a White Professor

CYNDI KERNAHAN

West Virginia University Press · Morgantown 2019

ISBN
Cloth 978-1-949199-23-9
Paper 978-1-949199-24-6
Ebook 978-1-949199-25-3

Library of Congress Cataloging-in-Publication Data
Names: Kernahan, Cyndi, author.
Title: Teaching about Race and Racism in the College Classroom : Notes
    from a White Professor / Cyndi Kernahan.
Description: Morgantown : West Virginia University Press, 2019 | Series:
    Teaching and Learning in Higher Education | Includes bibliographical
    references and index.
Identifiers: LCCN 2019024336 | ISBN 9781949199239 (cloth) | ISBN
    9781949199246 (paperback) | ISBN 9781949199253 (ebook)
Subjects: LCSH: College teaching–Social aspects–United States. | Race–
    Study and teaching–United States. | Racism–Study and teaching–
    United States. | Race relations–Study and teaching–United States. |
    Multicultural education–United States.
Classification: LCC LB2331 .K42 2019 | DDC 378.1/25–dc23
LC record available at https://lccn.loc.gov/2019024336

Book and cover design by Than Saffel / WVU Press
Cover illustrations by ddok / Shutterstock

For Suzanne Kernahan and Jerry Kernahan. You were the first to teach me that the world is not fair and the first to help me see my own responsibility in that.

CONTENTS

—

ACKNOWLEDGMENTS

—

AS A READER, I always like to read the acknowledgments. I want to get a better picture of the author. A more filled-out understanding of who they are and the people in their lives that have helped them to do what they do. For me, just as for most of us, that list is long, and I am sure I will forget and omit important people. I also know that there are people who have influenced me and assisted me in ways that I will never recognize.

First and foremost, I have to thank my students. For 20 years at the University of Wisconsin–River Falls, I have been teaching about racism and prejudice. My students have not only helped me learn how to teach, but they have also helped me learn more about race as they have generously shared their experiences and perspectives. I am grateful for the job I am privileged to do.

There are many, many others at the University of Wisconsin–River Falls that have helped me to write this book. First and foremost, several members of my department and the dean's office including Jody Sather, Kelly Duff-Bowers, and Donna Thompson. Todd Wilkinson and Melanie Ayres were kind enough to ask me about my writing and to talk with me about teaching on a regular basis. They are wonderful colleagues and friends. I am also especially indebted to Travis Tubrè. Travis has been my friend and steady colleague for nearly the entirety of my career at UWRF. As my department chair throughout this process, he has been unfailingly supportive and encouraging, even when it was hard for him to do so. I will always be grateful for his care and like-mindedness.

I am also especially grateful to Neil Kraus and Tricia Davis. Neil has been a consistent and encouraging fellow writer, helping me understand the process and encouraging me to keep at it even when I had no idea what I was doing. Without his well-timed and useful advice, I am quite certain I would not have received a contract to write this book. I am also grateful to Neil for our interesting conversations about education and the economy and for his thoughtful writing about both. Tricia Davis has been an incredibly supportive friend and colleague throughout my time at UWRF. She served as interim dean during the time I was writing this book, but despite her heavy schedule she still asked me about my writing and helped to push me forward when I felt worried or anxious.

As a teacher, it is so important to have colleagues with whom you can talk about teaching and from whom you can learn. I am lucky to have many such people in my life, including Ann Lawton, Arriety Lowell, Kevyn Juneau, and Veronica Justen. Those who teach about race make up a special subset of that group and I am lucky to have known or learned from many such teachers (on my own campus and from other institutions). These include Jennifer Willis-Rivera, Manu Sharma, Catherine Nasara, Jenn Sims, Norlisha Crawford, David Shih (an amazing writer about race), Erin Winkler, Chandra Waring, Lisa Wade, and Kim Case. Kim's writing and research proved especially valuable and I am grateful for her many contributions to our understanding of the teaching of privilege. Finally, Kevin Gannon, whose writing and presenting never fail to make me think about and question my own ideas and practices, has been an inspiring colleague.

There are many friends and colleagues from around the UW system whom I have been lucky enough to work with and who have helped me with this work. These include Regan Gurung, David Voelker, and Virginia Crank. Virginia was especially generous with her time and ideas, helping me to think about teaching and learning in ways both critical and compassionate. Her friendship and acceptance mean a lot to me.

Derek Krissoff and Jim Lang, the publisher and editor of this series, were extremely helpful and supportive throughout the book development process. From our initial conversation, through the revisions and rewrites, I always felt understood and supported. I am grateful for their help. Both were generous with their time and helpful in their comments, allowing me to feel more confident and competent. I am grateful as well to the anonymous reviewers. Their insightful and thoughtful comments were invaluable and truly helped to make the book so much better. Thanks, also, to the staff at West Virginia University Press for their important work.

Finally, I want to sincerely thank the people in my life who mean so much. My good friend Janie Eubanks, my partner in crime throughout graduate school who is still one of the smartest people I know. She has shown me what a smart and fierce intelligence can really look like. My good friends Rick Burgsteiner and Sandy Ellis have both been excellent conversation partners about race and racism and teaching. Rick helped me learn how to temper my strong opinions in a way that could make space for other people and their perspectives, an invaluable asset in teaching.

In addition to my friends, I am lucky to have some wonderful family. My parents, Jerry and Suzanne Kernahan, have always been my biggest fans and have let me know, always, how much they believe in me and my work. I am grateful as well for the wonderful children I have helped to raise, Nicolas Prince and Belle Force. Nicolas is an empathic and kind person who has helped me to better understand my students and the different forms that learning can sometimes take. I am proud of the adult he has become and grateful for the pride he has in me as his mother. Belle, a thoughtful, kind, and hard-working young woman, is my favorite college student to talk to and to learn from. I am not sure what I will do when she finishes college herself and I have no one left to learn the latest lingo and pop culture references from. Finally, and above all, I have to thank my wonderful husband Geoffrey Force. Geoff is the most consistently supportive and loving person I have ever known. He knows what I need and always works to take care of me when I need it most. He is also a remarkable thinker and conversation partner, helping me to sharpen my ideas and encouraging me to talk things out. I am grateful for his support during all the times I was sure I could not do this. Thank you, Geoff.

—

WHY IS IT SO HARD?

—

SEVERAL YEARS AGO, I was walking around campus with a good friend, lamenting how difficult the beginning of the semester can be. I was teaching my favorite course, the psychology of prejudice and racism, but many of the students were still in the very early stages of understanding. I was feeling a little frustrated and I told my friend that I was missing the students from the previous semester. The class had gone so well. I felt like we were really getting somewhere by the time it ended. Now, here I was, starting over again. He looked over at me and said, "It seems to me that you have to think of it like this: every semester you are taking a sledgehammer to a brand-new brick wall." No, I thought, my teaching is not like using a sledgehammer! And I certainly do not think of my students as a brick wall. Not at all. But he was certainly right that every semester is a new opportunity. Each one presents us with a chance to chip away at student understanding and to bring our students along into new ways of thinking—seeing problems, questions, texts, and examples in the ways that we do. Whatever your discipline, you have a way of thinking, a set of content knowledge, and a set of skills that you are hoping to impart to your students. You are reaching across the gap, from expert to novice, and hoping that your students will become excited and engaged as they begin to see your area of expertise in new and more complex ways.

If your teaching includes teaching about race and racism, those new ways of seeing take on added layers of emotional and cognitive complexity. Most students, just like everyone else, have pre-existing attitudes and feelings about race. They know what race means to them and they have an understanding of racism informed not only by the larger media, but also by their values, life experiences, and political beliefs. Because of students' pre-existing attitudes and feelings, teaching about race can be different from teaching about many other topics. Our beliefs and attitudes about race carry emotion and they are tied in to how we see ourselves morally and politically. In short, we have a lot to navigate as instructors. We are adding a scholarly understanding to something that is already personally meaningful and essential to a student's identity. Adding a new understanding, one that might potentially challenge or change that identity, is not a simple thing. It can threaten how students see themselves and how they fit into their families, their friend groups, and their communities.

Just to raise the stakes even more, we are living in a time of heightened racial tension in the United States overall. Since 2015, the share of Americans who believe that "race relations are generally bad" has outnumbered those believing that "race relations are generally good," reaching a new high of 72 percent in 2017 (Newport, 2017). Incidents of racial tension and harassment on college campuses have received widespread attention and instructors have found themselves at the center of race-based controversies as their comments (both on social media and in the classroom) are scrutinized and critiqued. Several instructors have been relieved of their teaching duties and some have lost their positions entirely.

It is in this environment of heightened scrutiny and tension that we walk into our classrooms, hoping to help our students understand race more clearly. However, as we will see in Chapter 1, there are substantial gaps between how we as instructors and experts understand race and the attitudes of many Americans, including our students. To give just one example, as I write this, a controversy has been swirling in the news about the causes of the U.S. Civil War. White House Chief of Staff John Kelly has argued publicly that the war was a failure of compromise, resulting because "honorable" people on both sides were unable to reach consensus (Astor, 2017). In the days that have followed this statement, historians and experts of the Civil War have challenged these assertions and pointed to the numerous compromises that *were* made in the lead up to the war. Furthermore, as historian and writer Jelani Cobb (2017) noted, White[1] supremacy as a motivator for all kinds of policy decisions in American history has been consistently downplayed and denied, resulting in an American public that has much less understanding of the role of racism in American history than is shown by the evidence.

In this atmosphere, where expert understanding differs from public understanding and where those in power perpetuate falsehoods around race, some instructors may find it easier to avoid race as a topic altogether. A few years ago, at one of those beginning-of-the-semester faculty parties that

---

1. In APA Style "White" and "Black" are capitalized as group names. I will capitalize them throughout as well, both because I use APA Style and because I feel capitalization honors how we use these words.

crowd the week before classes start, a professor of English told me that she was "done" with her ethnic film and literature course. At the time I was the coordinator of the ethnic studies program and I was hoping to get her course back into our offerings. She, however, let me know that there was no way that was going to happen. When I asked her why, she laughed and said it felt "impossible" to her. She talked about the resistance she faced from her mostly White students when she tried to get them to take seriously the themes of racism and discrimination that came up through the films and books the class discussed. She loved these films and books and wanted her students to begin to appreciate them as well, but the emotional toll was just too much. As someone who thought of herself as a caring and compassionate teacher, the discord and rancor were just too jarring and upsetting for her. She wanted a more positive teaching experience.

If you teach about racism, either as the main topic of a course or as a part of the course, you likely know how this instructor was feeling. And she isn't alone. Many teachers over the years have told me how they simply avoid "that part" of the course, the part regarding race and racism, or how they have "given up" on trying to convince their students (typically mostly White) that racism exists. As a first-year teacher of the psychology of prejudice and racism I found myself facing the same obstacles. I was mystified and shocked. How could they not see racism? Why did they question every piece of information I gave to them? Research supports that this kind of teaching is indeed difficult and that lower teaching evaluations and greater emotional turmoil can result, particularly for instructors of color (Boatright-Horowitz and Soeung, 2009; Sue, Rivera, Watkins, Kim, Kim, and Williams, 2011).

In response to these challenges, some instructors take a different approach. Rather than distancing themselves from race and racism in the classroom, these teachers become confrontational and sometimes even righteous in their work. Jane Elliott, the former third grade teacher from Riceville, IA, who created the "blue eyes-brown eyes" exercise and eventually became a nationally known diversity trainer, is perhaps the best-known example of this style of teaching. After teaching third graders, Elliott adapted her original methods of teaching children to teaching adults in corporate settings, giving workshops across the country. These workshops typically involved insults and anger directed at those who were arbitrarily (based on eye color and usually White) assigned to the low-power group. The point was to help these White people understand what it feels like to be a person of color, to feel the sting of oppression. Research, however, has shown that this program was largely ineffective in changing racial attitudes and may have created so much stress in the participants that they simply avoided learning more about race after the training (Wilson, 2011). Indeed, other work has typically shown that making participants feel blamed or guilty only leads to backlash, not learning or attitude change (Moss-Racusin, van der Toorn, Dovidio, Brescoll, Graham & Handelsman, 2014).

This book is about teaching race and racism in a way that is not blaming or shaming, a way that is compassionate but also relentlessly honest about the realities of racism and White supremacy in the United States. I believe that, at least in the classroom, we can confront the realities of racism without being confrontational. I also believe that we have to take care of ourselves and our students in ways that help us to avoid burning out and turning away from teaching about race altogether. Finding this path involves having a better understanding of what we are doing and the methods and mindsets that can help us do it. Using psychology, sociology, history, and the scholarship of teaching and learning (SoTL) across disciplines, I have identified several effective methods and mindsets and share them in this book. My goal is to both explain the evidence and translate it into strategies and ideas you can use in your own teaching. I will start with a focus on how we, as instructors, differ from our students in terms of our knowledge about race (Chapter 1), why students resist learning (Chapter 2), and understanding how to care for ourselves better (Chapter 3). The final three chapters of the book focus on creating a strong sense of belonging (Chapter 4), setting realistic expectations for learning (Chapter 5), and thinking through content choices (Chapter 6). Before digging in, I want to describe and elaborate on a theme that has come up repeatedly, and in different ways, as I have taught about racism myself and as I have researched this book: acceptance.

THE IMPORTANCE OF ACCEPTANCE

Accept That Learning Is Not a Linear Process

Diane Fallon, an English professor who includes race in her courses, refers to learning about race as "metastable." In describing her students, she says, "They truly are striving for complexity, but then revert to another position that feels more comfortably aligned with, or less challenging to, the value system and past experiences that they've brought with them to the classroom" (2006, p. 413). In my own teaching, I have seen this every semester. Just when I think everyone is starting to get the concept of institutional racism, for example, someone will make a comment or interpret a course reading in a way that tells me that they do not understand and cannot apply it to new examples. In some ways, this shouldn't be surprising. All learning appears to work in this way (Ambrose, Bridges, Lovett, DiPietro, & Norman, 2010). Moving from an understanding of race that is relatively simplistic toward one that is more complex is an emotional and cognitive challenge (more on this in Chapter 2) and so it is understandable that our students' learning will take time and that they may slip back into older, more familiar places along the way.

Accept Students, Even as They Resist Learning

In many ways, the relationship we have with our students is just as important as the content we are trying to teach. Learning is difficult and resistance to learning is a natural and normal part of the process (Brookfield, 2015). As an instructor, it is easy to feel frustration and sadness toward our students, particularly as we watch them revert to earlier understandings or reject the content. It is tempting, when this happens, to become focused on their resistance in a way that undermines our class atmosphere. We may become angry, sarcastic, or controlling, using our power as instructors to try and force learning. Or we may become passive and withdrawing, focused more on avoiding upset than teaching. In the chapters to come, I will focus on student resistance and instructor frustration, including steps we can take to better understand and predict our students' resistance while also protecting ourselves. For now, though, I will just say that I believe it helps to be as accepting as possible of the reality of learning. The process is going to be messy and meandering. It may feel good (at least temporarily) to try and force understanding and to be in control, but for students to learn they have to be the ones doing the work (Howard, 2015).

Accepting and allowing this messy back-and-forth is not always easy, but with some thought and intention, we can create classrooms that make space for this process.

Accept That Our Job Is Not to Compel Attitude Change

Many of us who teach about race do so because we care deeply about making the world better. As my colleague Christina Berchini put it in a recent interview, "I think part of that [her own teaching work] is inspired by a desperate desire to live in a better world for all people" (Lindquist, 2017). Many of us probably feel this way. We understand race in a way that many others do not, and we want everyone to see how racism works and to understand the enormous and unnecessary toll it takes. We can even see this with our own students. If you teach a course on race, I would guess that you have had at least one student tell you that he or she thinks all students should have to take your class, that everyone should be required to learn more about race. Having learned more about something that causes so much pain and so many problems, we want to share our understanding in the hopes of making change. In doing so as instructors, though, we have to be careful to remember our role. If we are trying to compel students to change their attitudes or behavior, we are not really accepting them where they are. Our message may be the same, we may still be presenting content we know to be true, but coercing is not the same as teaching. Teaching allows students to feel in control of their own learning (a key to motivation) and communicates that we care about them as people and not just as converts to our way of thinking.

To clarify this point further, it might help to contrast our teaching with other kinds of training. As educators, our course outcomes typically involve students demonstrating some understanding of content and then recalling and applying that content in some way. This is not the same as changing how they treat other people, how they vote, where they choose to live, or what policies they support. These kinds of complex behaviors are usually beyond the scope of our courses and though such behaviors can certainly be influenced by content knowledge, the relationship between understanding or knowledge and behavior is fuzzy and complicated by multiple factors. To put it another way, teaching about race is not the same thing as diversity training for employees. They are not unrelated, and, at times, I will use evidence from the training literature to inform my writing here, but such training is usually about compelling some employees to behave better and behavior change requires more than just awareness or knowledge. As research has shown, effective diversity training often includes structures for accountability and significant policy changes (Dobbin & Kalev, 2013). We can see this in the recent moves made by Starbucks in the wake of a high-profile incidence of racial profiling at one of their stores near Philadelphia (Starbucks, 2018). In their subsequent nationwide store trainings, Starbucks incorporated both employee awareness and policy changes to try and get their workers not only to understand racial bias but to behave differently as they followed new, and presumably fairer, store policies. As teachers, our mandate is usually more about understanding and awareness rather than setting up structures that compel behavioral change.

WHAT THIS BOOK IS ABOUT

If you are someone who teaches or is considering teaching about race and racism, this book is meant to help you do that. My focus will primarily be on *how* to teach rather than on *what* to teach. That is, I am assuming that if you have the ability to teach about race you already have a strong understanding of race and racism, particularly from your own disciplinary perspective. Concepts such as institutional racism, colorblindness, and racial privilege, to name just a few, will be referenced and defined briefly, but not described or discussed in detail. Instead, I will devote space to the teaching of race and to the difficulties such teaching presents. To be sure, I will provide citations and references throughout the book to excellent resources that could be used to learn more about race and racism, but the main focus will be on teaching and on how to support you as an instructor as you do this difficult work.

That said, and despite not focusing heavily on course content, I will focus in on the gaps in content knowledge and understanding that I believe are part of what make our teaching so difficult. Like many subject areas, there is often a wide gap between how experts view things and how novices view things (more on this in Chapter 1). I note this because I think that seeing this gap and focusing energy around trying to help students cross it is particularly helpful. When it comes to race, many Americans, including many of our students, have an understanding of race that is primarily rooted in their own personal experience. This idea manifests in a couple of assumptions: 1) the idea that racism is about individual bad behavior or unkindness (i.e., things I can see happening) and 2) the parallel belief that racism is something "good" people avoid so that only "bad" people are racist. This is very easy to see in our everyday language. For example, note the conversation that happens around shootings of unarmed Black men as some reporters and commentators ask repeatedly, "Was the shooter a racist?",

"Did you see him behaving in a racist way toward people of color?" The assumption seems to be that knowing the answer to this question ("Was he a racist?") will provide an answer as to how this event happened. If the person was "good" and not a racist, then there must be some other explanation. If they were "bad" and racist, then we can attribute the incident simply to that person's prejudice. If it is just about one person, then our society will not have to contend with the larger currents of racism and White supremacy that underlie such incidents. We will not have to consider solutions beyond just getting rid of those few "bad apples."

Most experts know that race is more complicated than just individual racial prejudice. We know that we all hold racial biases, even if unintentionally, because of our racially biased environments and institutions. We see the bad barrels in addition to, or instead of just, the bad apples. We also understand the embedded and sometimes unseen nature of race and how racism plays a part in our culture, our institutions, our laws, our policies, and our norms. Finally, we can (sometimes) more easily see and understand our own racial biases, knowing that they are a part of our own socialization into a larger system. Understanding all of this means that we understand a lot of important content that enriches and expands our perspectives because it moves us beyond just our own individual and personal experiences. I trust that you know this foundational content and my goal is to help you teach in a way that helps you help your students. In the pages that follow, I focus less on what that content should be and more on how to effectively help students grapple with it so that they can begin to develop their own more complicated and nuanced perspectives on race.

Finally, I want to make a distinction between teaching about race and teaching in a way that is inclusive across race.

Inclusive pedagogy or inclusive teaching involves being attentive to the identities of our students and deliberately creating classrooms that are welcoming and allow equal access to learning across those identities (Center for Research on Learning and Teaching, 2016). Such teaching is, of course, imperative for students marginalized by race and important for all students. It can sound obvious, but it is remarkable how often inclusive teaching is not part of the conversation on teaching and not something that is focused on in terms of improving student retention and success (Gannon, 2018). In this book, my focus is on teaching about race rather than on inclusive teaching per se, but I do include ideas that are a part of inclusive teaching. The latter half of the book is concentrated on strategies for increasing feelings of belonging, setting expectations, and using content in ways that help students feel included. One example of inclusive teaching that is a part of the book concerns the distinctions between how White students and students of color are likely to experience our classrooms. In making such distinctions, I try to be aware of and sensitive to the different lived realities that students of color bring to our classrooms and the ways that this difference can influence the learning and experience of these students, particularly with a White instructor and White classmates. That said, however, this book is not primarily a book on inclusive teaching or inclusive pedagogy. Instead, it is more about race and racism and how to teach these topics effectively and with compassion for the student experience.

MY OWN PERSPECTIVE

Finally, it is important to be upfront about who I am and the experiences and education that inform my writing. I am a social psychologist and my work in recent years has been primarily the scholarship of teaching and learning (SoTL). I draw from both the social psychological literature and the SoTL literature to inform my teaching practice. Both have been invaluable in developing the larger philosophy of teaching about race that I share with you here. I am also a White, straight, female instructor who teaches primarily White students at a small public university in the Midwest. And while a lot of faculty are similar to me, especially in terms of race (e.g., 76 percent of all college instructors are White according to 2016 data from National Center for Education Statistics, McFarland et al., 2018), I also understand that my experience is limited. As a White person, I do not have the visceral and lived experience of racism that my colleagues and students of color have. There are other limitations too: the size of my classes (30 or fewer mostly), the Whiteness of my students (86 percent at UW River Falls), and the relatively conservative politics of my campus.

In trying to get outside my own narrow perspective, I have taken several approaches. First, I have tried to learn more about the experiences of my colleagues of color and will include them throughout the book where possible. In addition to individual experiences, I have gathered research on the experiences of teaching about race as an instructor of color and I share that work here. Given the reality of racism in the United States, teaching in general and teaching about race in particular are different for people of color than for White people and I try to be clear about that throughout the book. I hope that the perspectives, evidence, and information I provide will be of use to all instructors, but I am aware that my own perspective is limited.

To get outside my own classroom, I also frequently give presentations on race and bias to larger groups of students, faculty, and community members. Some of these presentations have occurred on my own campus, but most have not. These talks have allowed me to work with larger and more heterogeneous audiences, thus expanding my understanding and further testing my ideas. In doing this, I not only get to experience the responses and reactions of people who are not my own students, but I also get to meet other people who are doing the kinds of teaching I am doing and to hear about the challenges they face. One recent example of this for me was discussing the teaching of racism with a colleague from a much smaller, more politically liberal campus on the West Coast. For her, resistance to learning about race comes in ways that are very different from mine. Rather than resisting the realities of institutional racism, her students often resist her measured and evidence-based approach. They want her to be more of an activist, less of a teacher. By reaching out to others who teach about race or reading about their experiences, I have tried to broaden my understanding of the challenges we face and the ways in which we can use evidence to meet such challenges.

Finally, I am deeply committed to understanding the teaching process generally and to using good evidence and theory to inform and improve that process. As a part-time faculty developer, I have the privilege of working with instructors from across disciplines and on a variety of teaching issues. This work has helped me to read more widely in the teaching and SoTL literatures and confirmed my belief that through research and the gathering of evidence about teaching, we can improve and learn from one another. In this book I will try to share what I know in the hope that it will help you along the way.

Chapter 1

NAÏVE UNDERSTANDINGS: HOW WE DIFFER FROM OUR STUDENTS

—

IN MAY OF 2015, an incoming professor of sociology and African American studies at Boston University, Saida Grundy, suddenly found herself in the midst of a Twitter controversy (Hetter, 2015). Nick Pappas, a college student at another university and founder of SoCawlege.com, a conservative website for students, found and republished several of Dr. Grundy's tweets about race. For example, one tweet asks "why is white america [*sic*] so reluctant to identify White college males as a problem population?" Putting these remarks in context, 2014 had seen the killing deaths of Eric Garner, Michael Brown, and Tamir Rice while early 2015 had seen the killing deaths of Walter Scott and Freddie Gray, all at the hands of law enforcement. Each of these high-profile deaths was accompanied by weeks of protest that reignited again when the officers involved were acquitted or were not charged. Race and the demand for racial justice was in the air and soon there would be protests on college campuses across the country.

Over the course of the next week or so, numerous tweets, blog posts, and stories were written in response to Dr. Grundy's comments. As CNN reported, some referred to her as a "racist professor" and wondered how she might ever fairly teach the White college men that would certainly be among her students (Hetter, 2015). A petition appeared online as well, with about 200 people signing on to ask that her tenure-track position at Boston University, set to begin that fall 2015, be revoked. At the same time, Dr. Grundy had numerous supporters with about 2,000 signing a petition in her defense. Other sociologists noted that her comments were relatively uncontroversial and that many of her statements were empirically supportable. Speaking to *Inside Higher Ed* (Flaherty, 2015), Tressie McMillan Cottom, a sociologist at Virginia Commonwealth University, noted that Dr. Grundy was using "inside" language in an "outside" context; that is, speaking as a sociologist while tweeting to a general audience. Her expertise may have seemed obvious to those with similar training, but to an outside audience that expertise was invisible. She just seemed like a "biased" professor who would be unable to teach fairly. This case is of course about more than just a gap in expertise—the race of the instructor matters as does the larger political context—but for now, I want to focus us in on that gap as a way to think about our teaching challenges more broadly.

WHAT IS EXPERTISE?

The gap between "inside" and "outside" language is at the heart of all expertise, and really, of all teaching. Any expert in any field will always have a denser and more complex network of information and understanding compared to a novice (Ambrose, Bridges, DiPietro, Lovett, & Norman, 2010). Communicating across this gap is the job of all teachers, but the problem can be especially challenging for those of us whose expertise involves race. How can there be expertise when it comes to something like race, something that can be so personal in terms of attitudes and experiences and something that elicits such strong feelings?

Consider the Starbucks #RaceTogether campaign that CEO Howard Schultz launched in March of 2015. The idea of the campaign was to get people to talk about race. Baristas were asked to strike up conversations with their customers (using stickers placed on coffee cups), and a list of facts about race was published in *USA Today* to encourage further conversation among all Americans. The premise of the campaign, launched in the midst of ongoing protests around police shootings of unarmed Black men, was the idea that if everyone talked and shared their differing perspectives around race we would understand each other better and the conflict would ebb. As many critics pointed out at the time, however, the matter of perspective was left unresolved. Whose perspective would be taken seriously? Who would be believed? And as Cottom (2015) asked: Is the customer always right? The inherent power differences between baristas and customers, not to mention the time pressures of people grabbing coffee on their way to work, would seem to make any meaningful talk unlikely.

Another problem for the campaign was the assumption that talking about race, any kind of talking about race, would lead to understanding. As those of us who teach about race understand, there is a difference between *talking* about race and *learning* about race. When the campaign began, I was asked, because I am a teacher of race, to appear on a local radio call-in show to discuss the campaign (WPR, 2015). During the show, I argued that talking about race can be difficult and that those who are trained to teach about race might be needed if the goal was real understanding. Given the long history of racism in our country and the many misconceptions that people have about race, it would be helpful to have an expert to guide the discussion. Many callers did not agree, dismissing the idea that any particular expertise was necessary.

Imagine this same scenario if the topic was finance. We have plenty of societal concerns around money and most everyone has a lot of personal experience with money, but would anyone seriously propose simply talking about financial problems or getting the perspective of strangers as a way to solve these problems? Unlike with race, most people seem to agree that some people have expertise in this area (economists, financial advisors) and that their expertise is different from and moves beyond just their own personal experience. We trust them to have dispassionate, "objective" ideas. We may not like their recommendations or opinions, but we typically do not question their expertise in the same way, dismissing that such expertise is possible in the first place.

In some ways it is easy to understand why students and others shrug off the idea of expertise when it comes to race. People *do* have different levels of experience with race and that experience matters. According to the Pew Research Center (2016), there are broad differences in how different racial groups perceive our society. Black Americans are much more likely to agree that the country still has work to do to achieve racial equality (88 percent) as compared to Whites (53 percent). Similarly, when asked how fairly Blacks are treated across several specific situations, the majority of Black Americans feel that their group receives unfair treatment at the hands of police (84 percent), in the courts (75 percent), when applying for loans (66 percent), and in the workplace (64 percent). Only half (50 percent) of White Americans believe that this is true for the police and the percentages are lower for every other category of treatment when it comes to how they believe Black Americans experience society. Overall, White Americans are just much more skeptical about the realities of racism and much less likely to believe that discrimination occurs or that it is a major factor in the lives of Black Americans. In some ways these numbers represent the extremes of difference, as Blacks and Whites are (usually) the most disparate in terms of attitudes. But if we dig deeper into the numbers to include Hispanics and Asian Americans, we still see the same pattern: Whites see things as better for people of color than the people of color themselves (Binder, 2014; Pew Research, 2016).

Despite these clear differences, however, there are also limitations when it comes to understanding race and racism only through personal experience. The lived, visceral experience of racism is powerful and important, but it may not help individuals to clearly see and name the larger, more structural ways in which racism operates. Students who are Black, Latinx, or Asian American surely know that racism is a problem, and that it is a large problem, but understanding the specifics of institutional and cultural forms of racism often requires additional learning that goes beyond what is taught in our individualistic American culture (Jones, 1996). To see what I mean, consider some of the other findings from that same Pew Research Report (2016) as well as the findings of a fascinating series of reports by NPR in 2017. These large attitude surveys found that most Americans believe discrimination resulting from individual prejudice is a bigger problem than discrimination built into laws and government policies. This was true for nearly every racial group surveyed, including half or more of African Americans, Latinos, Whites, and Asian Americans. The only exceptions to this pattern were Native Americans and Latino Immigrants (see the whole series of reports to learn more).

Given my own training in the sociology and psychology of race, it is hard to see the findings of these surveys and not feel disheartened. It is clear to me that discrimination built into laws and policies is the bigger problem. Indeed, you could argue that lessening institutional forms of racial discrimination is the fastest way to eliminate individual prejudice. As Ibram Kendi points out in his excellent 2016 book *Stamped from the Beginning* racist ideas are a result of racist discrimination. They are produced as a way to justify racist policies. Changing those policies to make them anti-racist is probably the best way to decrease racist thinking and the prejudice that goes along with it. I suspect that most experts on race from across disciplines (e.g., psychology, sociology, history) would agree. The norms of a polite society might sometimes constrain individual prejudice, but bias that happens systematically is ever-present and often much harder to detect and to stop precisely because it is built into our institutions and laws. Furthermore, we are often unable to see the biases we hold and the ways in which they influence our behavior (Banaji & Greenwald, 2013). Finally, it can also be hard to separate institutional from individual when it comes to our perceptions. We behave according to the norms of our institutions and we carry out the laws and policies of our government in ways that exacerbate racial inequality even as we feel that we are endorsers of equality and fairness.

This difference in understanding does not mean that

those of us who study race do not see the importance of individual prejudice or that the personal experiences of our students, especially our students of color, are unimportant. It just means that we see that racism does not begin or end with individual prejudice. Being able to see and clearly articulate both the institutional and the individual levels of racism is helpful for several reasons. First, we can situate ourselves and see how our own experiences fit within a larger framework of privilege or disadvantage based on race. We can also get beyond the belief that racism is about being either a "good" or a "bad" person. We know that individual experience is limited, and that good people can still benefit from racism and enforce racist ideas just by following the norms or policies or our society. Moving from a simpler and more personalized understanding of race to one that can encompass both personal experiences and the forces of history, institution, and culture is not easy, but it is a key move. As students make this move, they should be able to see past limited morality-based reasoning and toward a more nuanced understanding. They too will be able to clearly name what racism is and how it works, helping them make sense of such a big problem. We made this move and developed this understanding ourselves at one point and it is our job to help our students do the same, even as we recognize how difficult it can be and that each of them will have a slightly different starting point.

Throughout the book, I will refer back to this gap as a way to remember how we likely differ from our students. I will use the words "individual" racism and "institutional" racism as a way to shorthand what I mean, but another way to conceptualize it using terminology from my field of psychology is the difference between prejudice and racism. Prejudice is an individual emotion or attitude (Tatum, 2017).

It represents a person's feelings toward a particular social group or toward another individual based on a group membership (race, gender, etc.). Racism informs racial prejudice, of course, but racism is a much larger force. Racism encompasses the larger set of advantages or disadvantages faced by each racial group, operating at individual, institutional, and cultural levels to influence us (Jones, 1996; Tatum, 2017). Racism also includes and explains the opportunity and outcome gaps we see for nearly every societal measure: educational attainment, employment, wealth, life expectancy, and so on. This dynamic and complex system of advantage and disadvantage is what we, as experts, are often talking about when we talk about racism, but this is not what most Americans, our students included, think about when they think about racism. Instead, most Americans focus on prejudice, on the individual acts of unkind behavior or expressions of stereotyped thinking.

Erin Winkler, an associate professor of African American studies at the University of Wisconsin–Milwaukee, described this gap in her 2018 report on her students' learning. For her research, she examined how students learned about racism and she described racism (again, conceptualized here institutionally and systematically rather than individually) as a "threshold concept." Threshold concepts are those course concepts that are both difficult to learn but also transformative. In the words of Winkler: "racism as a system of advantage based on race is *the* concept students must truly 'get' in order to move forward in the class" (pp. 1–2, emphasis original). At the start of the course, none of her students understood racism in this way, but as the semester progressed, they increasingly crossed over the threshold. Her tracking of their progress tells us a few important things about the learning process. First, most students were able to develop at least some understanding of racism as institutional and systemic. Nearly 90 percent had done so by the midterm. Furthermore, both White students and students of color (who were a little more than 40 percent of the sample) failed to understand racism as a system of advantage on the first day, but students of color tended to learn more quickly than White students. Students of color reached her rubric-based benchmarks of understanding at a faster pace and their comments reinforced their growing awareness of institutional racism. At the end of the course, students of color were also the most likely to have achieved the highest levels of understanding. In this difference, we can see an important nuance when it comes to racial identity and understanding: being a person of color does not guarantee that you will understand what racism is or how it operates at an institutional level, but it certainly lends itself to easier and quicker understanding. Furthermore, as Winkler notes, "this shift [to a more system-based perspective] may be more difficult for students whose sense of self may potentially be troubled by this shift" (p. 13). In other words, White students often struggle as they come to terms with the advantages of their race precisely because they are advantaged by race. Resisting the implications of that advantage will be an important part of Chapter 2. In that chapter, I will focus on resistance for both White students and students of color.

In the remainder of this chapter, I will highlight what we know about American's racial attitudes. I do this as a way to help you better understand what students are likely to believe as they enter our courses. First, though, I want to reiterate how liberating it can be for students (or anyone really) to cross over the threshold of understanding when it comes to racism. The idea that racism is mostly about personal prejudice may seem easy: just get rid of the "bad" and racist people and the problem is solved, but it can also be personally indicting. What if I say the wrong thing? What if I have racist ideas in my head? Does this make me one of the "bad" people? When I teach, I usually ask students on the first day to write down and discuss their biggest fears (as well as hopes) for the coming semester. The most common response I hear is the fear of saying the wrong thing and/ or finding out that they themselves are "racist." This seems to happen most often with White students, but students of color can have this fear as well. As the class progresses and the students discover that racism is actually a larger force and that it influences much of society, it is disconcerting and upsetting, but it is also freeing. Understanding our own prejudices and biases as part of a larger framework gives us permission to talk about them and to see beyond the moralistic framework of "good" and "bad" people. It also provides a framework and language that can help students make better sense of their own experiences when it comes to racism and prejudice.

THE AMERICAN BELIEF IN COLORBLINDNESS

Colorblindness is the relatively simple idea that if we ignore or avoid noticing race then racial discrimination will cease to be a problem. Colorblindness rests on two simplistic notions: 1) the notion of an individual, and not institutional, racism as described above, and 2) the notion that all our thinking about race is fully conscious and controlled (without implicit or automatic components). If racism is simply a matter of personal, voluntary belief and behavior then colorblindness becomes a natural solution: all that is needed is for each of us to ignore race and racism ceases to be a problem. As noted by Apfelbaum, Norton, and Sommers (2012) the ideology of colorblindness permeates our legal, educational, and criminal justice systems and the consequences are harmful. As these authors note, striving toward colorblindness typically makes our institutions more, not less, racially biased.

One famous example of this comes from the U.S. Supreme Court's Chief Justice John Roberts. He wrote in 2007 that the way "to stop discrimination on the basis of race is to stop discriminating on the basis of race" (as cited in Apfelbaum et al., 2012, p. 205). In that particular case the court struck down a desegregation plan that allowed the schools in Louisville, Kentucky, and Seattle, Washington, to use race in determining students' school placement. Research has shown that without such racially conscious plans in place most schools become, and are, quite segregated by race (Hannah-Jones, 2014). Colorblind policies allow our institutional and unconscious biases to shape our outcomes. Nevertheless, colorblindness continues to be the dominant racial ideology within the United States and many Americans seem to believe that the racial playing field is already fair. Avoiding talk about or noticing race are all that we need to maintain that equality.

Nowhere is the belief in colorblindness more widespread than when it comes to younger generations of Americans. Much has been written about the so-called millennial generation and the argument usually goes like this: millennials (roughly defined as those born after 1980 through about 1996), along with the generations that follow, are colorblind. That is, they have been raised during a time of relative racial equality and are beyond racial bias. They do not notice race or hold negative stereotypes. The hope seems to be that as the older, "racist" cohorts die off, younger Americans will usher in a new post-racial society. Even Oprah Winfrey supported this notion, stating in an interview with the BBC that "they just have to die" in reference to older Whites who harbor racist views (Desmond-Harris, 2015).

In 2014, MTV conducted a large national survey of racial attitudes among young people aged 14–24 including all racial groups. The survey was part of a larger media campaign (Binder, 2014) designed to help younger people think more about their own racial biases and to "erase the hidden . . . bias all around us." The survey results for all racial groups revealed a strong belief in both equality (91 percent endorsed the belief that everyone should be treated equally) and color-blindness: 74 percent of Whites and 72 percent of people of color agreed that society would be better off if we were truly colorblind and never considered race or ethnicity. Also, and in keeping with the belief that they represent something new, 72 percent said that they believed their generation is less racially biased than older Americans and that as their generation grows into leadership roles, racism will become less of an issue for the country (58 percent).

While millennials are indeed a more racially diverse generation, about 43 percent non-White as compared to 28 percent non-White for the baby boomers (Pew Research, 2015), the racial attitudes of White millennials are not that different. General Social Survey research has shown that White millennials are just as likely as older Whites to say that Blacks are less hardworking (31 percent) and less intelligent (23 percent) than Whites (as cited in Wade, 2015). Similarly, implicit pro-White racial bias is remarkably similar across the generations, with no significant differences between younger and older Whites (Nosek et al., 2007). Overall, the main difference between younger generations of White people and older ones may simply be their *belief* that they are less biased.

Young people of color are also very similar to their older

counterparts in terms of both attitude and experience. For example, young people of color reported more discrimination based on race than young Whites did. According to the survey done by MTV (Binder, 2014), 33 percent said they had been treated differently by a teacher because of their race as compared to just 13 percent of Whites. Similarly, about 65 percent of young people of color agree that Whites receive more opportunities as compared to racial minority groups (only 39 percent of young Whites agree with this statement). At the same time, however, there is a strong belief in colorblindness, hard work, and the individual ability to rise above racial discrimination. As noted above, young people of color strongly agree that not considering race at all would improve society. McElwee (2015) also found that when he examined data from the American National Election Survey more than 40 percent of young Blacks (17–34) agreed with the statement that Blacks could be as well off as Whites if they worked harder (a slightly higher percentage than that found for older Blacks). These seemingly paradoxical findings, experiencing more discrimination yet believing in colorblindness and the individual ability to overcome discrimination, are not that different from those of older Americans of color. The Pew Research Center (2010; 2013; 2016) has consistently shown that those who are Black or Hispanic simultaneously report greater experience with discrimination as compared to Whites while also downplaying the role that racial discrimination (especially institutional discrimination) plays in affecting life outcomes. My suspicion, based on the findings I shared earlier about the lack of understanding around institutional racism, is that these young people simply lack the language and framework needed to see racism in all its forms and to put a name to their experiences.

Finally, our belief in colorblindness informs one other set of findings about American racial attitudes that I think is important for better understanding our students as well as our larger political environment. The social psychologists Michael Norton and Samuel Sommers (2011) asked both Black and White Americans to report their perceptions of anti-Black and *anti-White* bias. The participants were asked to report how much they thought Blacks and Whites were the victims of discrimination for each decade from the 1950s through the 2000s using a scale from 1 to 10. The results were fascinating. First, those who were Black perceived a gradual decline in anti-Black bias over time and small levels of anti-White bias that only increased slightly in the 1990s and 2000s. For Whites, however, the perception included an interesting crossover effect. Most Whites perceived that anti-Black bias dropped sharply from the 1970s through the 2000s with anti-White bias rising sharply and exceeding that for anti-Black bias beginning in the 1990s and 2000s. Keep in mind that these numbers do not reflect actual racial biases (in terms of employment, housing, education, etc.) or survey numbers taken over time, but rather the perception of bias as participants believe it to have changed and shifted over time. For White respondents, it is almost as if anti-White racial bias rose in response to perceived decreases in anti-Black bias. As the authors of the study note, Whites seem to see "racism as a zero-sum game that they are now losing" (Norton & Sommers, 2011, p. 215).

Here again we see the mismatch between expert and novice understandings of race. When viewed through the lens of institutional and cultural racism, the perception that anti-White bias is rising can seem nonsensical. There is no evidence that bias against Whites is a problem. From education, to housing, to health care, criminal justice, wages, and wealth, every part of American society works in a way that advantages Whites over other racial groups (Gallagher, 2011; Pew Research, 2016). But for many Americans, socialized to think in terms of colorblindness and individual (rather than institutional) racial bias, White racial advantages are largely invisible or simply denied.

These findings have been replicated across several national polls. First, the MTV poll cited earlier (Binder, 2014) found that about 48 percent of young Whites and 27 percent of young people of color agreed with the statement "discrimination against Whites is now as big a problem as discrimination against racial minorities." Similarly, the 2015 American Values survey conducted by the Public Religion Research Institute asked participants how much they agreed with the statement "discrimination against Whites has become as big a problem as discrimination against Blacks and other minorities." This broad national survey found that about 43 percent of all Americans agreed with the statement while 55 percent disagreed (Jones, Cox, Cooper, & Lienesch, 2015). White people who identified as Republican (64 percent) and working class (60 percent) were more likely to agree with the statement than were those who identified as Democrats (28 percent) or those with a college degree (38 percent). Finally, an NPR poll published in 2017 found that 55 percent of Whites (74 percent if Republican and 65 percent if without a college degree) believed that there is discrimination against White people. These same respondents were unlikely to identify specific instances of personal discrimination based on being White (ranging from 1–32 percent across a variety of situations), but they still believe it to be an overall problem.

Given that colorblindness is so pervasive, it really is not surprising that so many Americans (mostly White but including some people of color) believe in a rising anti-White bias. In an environment that prizes and normalizes color-blindness, the mere mention of race or racism can be read as a threat. Colorblindness rests on the assumption that racism is a matter of individual bias and personal morality so that those who are "good" avoid noticing or discussing it. Indeed, research has shown that people, including Whites and people of color, will go to great lengths to avoid mentioning race even when that behavior is personally costly (Apfelbaum, Sommers, & Norton, 2008; Pauker, Apfelbaum, & Spitzer, 2015). Why? Because mentioning or noticing races violates the norms of colorblindness and suggests you might harbor racial bias.

As an example of how colorblindness can lead to feelings of anti-White bias, consider recent national events. The 2014 killings of several unarmed Black men at the hands of police (most notably Michael Brown, Eric Garner, and Tamir Rice) sparked a lot of discussion, news coverage, and activism around race and racism (e.g., Black Lives Matter). For those who understand institutional racism and the extent of implicit racial bias, these killings were upsetting but not surprising. We understand that these kinds of killings happen routinely; only the news coverage and protests were new. However, for those without this understanding, the news coverage and protests were an unwelcome intrusion. As racism's role in the police killings was discussed and debated, anger and backlash increased (e.g., police lives matter, all lives matter). In our colorblind context, bringing up race and racism as an explanation for police behavior was transformed into a *bias* against police and a *bias* against Whites. If both "sides" (e.g., police and Black activists) are assumed to be equal in power and opportunity, then bringing up race is unfair and thought to be "racist" on the part of those doing the protesting. It is bemoaned as "playing the race card."

This is how colorblind assumptions (everything is equal so long as we ignore race) facilitate feelings of anti-White bias.

In the classroom, assumptions of colorblindness pop up routinely, particularly as learning is just beginning. Early one semester, a student of mine, writing a discussion post online, equated the Black Lives Matter movement to the KKK. He was arguing that "both sides" had misperceptions and had done bad things. These organizations, of course, are not at all the same. The KKK is a domestic terror group and Black Lives Matter is a decentralized social justice movement. But if you can see his thinking through the lens of colorblind assumptions, it makes sense. If you have been raised to believe that colorblindness is the norm and you do not yet understand the extent of racism—the wide institutionalized disparities that our history and policies create—then a simplistic equating of these groups might not sound far off. They become, in this colorblind world, two organizations with relatively equal power favoring their own racial group. This is wrong, of course, and I want to be clear that I am not saying that this perception should not be corrected. I was quick to post back with a matter-of-fact explanation and citations to each groups' goals and statements about themselves. But by understanding the origins of his statement, I think I was able to respond with more clarity, less anger, and in a way that (I hope) addressed the broader misperceptions driving his comment. This student went on to be a great participant in class and I believe, based on his work, that he learned a lot by the end of the course. But his assumptions at the beginning of the class clearly reflected a lot of misinformation about race and racism.

In this example and in so many more, we can see that colorblind ideology makes the classroom a more difficult and treacherous place for teachers of race. Saida Grundy, the instructor whose story began this chapter, describes this problem as one of racial illiteracy. In August of 2015, several months after her Twitter comments were brought to public attention and she found herself the subject of controversy, Dr. Grundy began her career as an assistant professor at Boston University. In an interview with *Inside Higher Ed,* Grundy described her experience with the controversy and her disappointment at the ways in which her field (sociology) is often misconstrued as "people who have a set of opinions" rather than a field of scholars who hold expertise (Jaschik, 2015). She also said, "I have tried to explain to myself . . . that the country is very race-illiterate. Just like we have a problem with science literacy, we have a problem with race literacy." Moving our students toward race literacy and away from colorblindness is the goal for most of us, including Dr. Grundy, who now teaches undergraduate and graduate classes on race and ethnicity.

RECOMMENDATIONS AND SUGGESTIONS

Given the evidence presented above, it is likely that your students will be: 1) thinking about racism as personal prejudice rather than as systemic or institutional, 2) subscribers to the notion of colorblindness, 3) convinced that young people are less biased, and 4) concerned that perhaps anti-White bias is growing. These beliefs will not be the norm for all students, of course, and depending on the demographics of your students and your campus culture, these may be more or less descriptive. Nevertheless, given the evidence of the extent of racial bias and the pervasiveness of colorblind racial ideology, it is likely that these beliefs will characterize the thinking of many of your students in both obvious and not-so-obvious ways. Below are two suggestions for how to accept your students with compassion while also holding to the evidence-based truth about race and racism.

Accept Their Starting Point

If we as instructors can accept our students' initial beliefs, I believe we can be more sensitive, and ultimately, more effective. Being sensitive does not mean that we do not expect them to learn or to work with challenges, but rather that we understand where they are starting and how that may differ from our own perspective. In our courses, we are asking students to set aside feelings that the world is colorblind and fair to accept a world that is much more racially biased and unfair. Even more difficult, we are asking them to move from an understanding of racial bias that is primarily personal to one that is cultural and institutional, a way of thinking about racism that implicates us all. This is an important move and one that can free us from the notion that people are either "good (racially unbiased)" or "bad (racist)." But making this move also forces our students to let go of the belief that as long as they themselves are colorblind they cannot be bad people. Through our teaching, we are taking away that easy path and helping them to see instead the larger and largely out-of-their-individual-control reality of how racism works and the ways in which it shapes us all.

To accept their starting point really just means that we are both patient and persistent in the face of student misperceptions. Race is not taught particularly well in most K–12 settings (Loewen, 2018) and its teaching has been under attack in many others (see the ban on Mexican American studies in Arizona schools as just one example). Should it be surprising that so many students do not understand how pervasive racism is? How it works institutionally? It is unlikely that most students (though not all) are willfully ignoring a broader understanding of racism. Instead, they are carrying the misinformation that most Americans hold. Luckily, there is psychological research on how to persist in the face of misinformation more generally and we can use that research to inform our teaching.

In a review of the literature, Stephan Lewandowsky, Ullrich Ecker, Colleen Seifert, Norbert Schwarz, and John Cook (2012) summarize how and why misinformation persists, but they also point to several evidence-based strategies for correcting misinformation. Most relevant for us as instructors is the technique of providing an alternative narrative while avoiding repetition of the misinformation. First, it is important to understand that the reason misinformation persists, according to the authors, is because it is part of a larger story. As an example, colorblindness is a large and persistent story when it comes to race in the United States. As noted above, colorblindness is accepted by most Americans as the right way to deal with racism, and the assumptions that underlie colorblindness (everything is fair and equal now, there are no hidden or systematic biases) are well accepted. Digging even deeper, you may recognize that these ideas are part of an even larger American story, the notion of inevitable progress, that the United States is always getting "better," particularly around race (Loewen, 2018). In this story, colorblindness makes sense: bringing up race pushes us backward and disrupts inevitable racial progress.

According to Lewandowsky and his colleagues, the way to get past this narrative is to do two things. First, we have to repeatedly provide a new, alternative story. In the case of teaching about race, that story is one of institutional and systematic racial bias. Second, we have to ignore or at least minimize the colorblind story rather than explicitly pointing it out and engaging with it each time it is raised. In practice, I think this means not continually rehashing the existence of racism itself. "Is racism real?" is not a useful question and "debating" it means engaging with the premises of the story of colorblindness as if they could be true. As if it is possible that everything is fair and equal now and there are no implicit and institutional biases. According to the research, engaging with misinformation directly inadvertently strengthens peoples' belief in that misinformation. In our case, this means that repeatedly engaging with the notion of colorblindness as a possible reality means unintentionally strengthening students' belief in it.

Instead, the misinformation research suggests that we would do better to ignore the question "Is racism real?" and instead focus on defining racism more in line with our scholarly understanding, coming back to that new definition and story repeatedly. It is likely (and to be expected) that students will revert to their misconceptions throughout the course but ignoring those misconceptions rather than fighting them repeatedly while also reinforcing our new story and tying new pieces of content into that new story should improve learning.

You may have to think through your own course a bit to see the other stories and narratives that are specific to your content, the notions that you feel like you are continually debunking. Once you find them, try to construct an alternative story that can become your go-to narrative. Rather than arguing the point, try instead to deflect and redirect into the new story. Of course, there will be times when student resistance will make that difficult. My guess, though, is that most of the time you can simply sidestep the wrongheaded notions they bring to class or post in discussions while emphasizing new evidence and a new story. It is easy to believe that we need to confront misinformation head on each and every time it appears, but that only leads us into the trap of reiterating misinformation and inadvertently strengthening it. The research suggests that ignoring misinformation while repeatedly emphasizing a new story grounded in the evidence you are providing will be much more effective. To go back to the example I mentioned above, it was tempting, when my student posted that the KKK was the equivalent of Black Lives Matter on our discussion board, to bring this up explicitly in class and make a big deal of debunking it in front of others. But looking back, that only would have engaged with misinformation (and perhaps embarrassed the student). I think it was better to simply provide the alternative evidence to that student (and available for others to read on the discussion board if they happened to see it) and to use precious class time to focus on more substantive questions about the content. The idea is to build the new story you want them to learn rather than engaging with the old fiction over and over again.

Every instructor I know has a list of the myths or wrongheaded ideas that plague their classes and disciplines from learning styles to climate change to creationism to chemical imbalances that cause mental illness. One writing instructor I know introduced me to a whole book on the subject, *Bad Ideas About Writing* (Ball & Loewe, 2017). Perusing the table of contents, I realized how difficult it must be to teach writing and to teach future teachers about writing given how many mythical and simplistic ideas about writing are out there, including the notion that good writers are just born that way and that students should be taught never to use the word "I." In all of these cases, deflecting or completely avoiding the myth is really the key thing to remember. And really, it is probably easier than we might imagine. Students may bring these ideas up, but most of the time it is probably us, as instructors, who raise and then debunk the myths. We know how common they are, and we sometimes enjoy puncturing these outdated or upsetting ideas. We would do better to try to think about, in advance, the misinformation and misconceptions that students are likely to bring and then figure out what our alternative story will be and how we can continually reinforce it throughout the class. Being mindful of how we are inadvertently engaging with old ideas and emphasizing the new story rather than the old one should help our students learn.

Make Your Expertise Explicit and Affirm Theirs

Unlike other kinds of content areas, students will probably not assume that you have expertise or scholarly knowledge about race. Because of this, you will want to be clear about what qualifies you to teach about race and how it fits into your particular discipline and training. It may seem strange to have to spell this out (would we ask a physicist to tell us why she is qualified to teach astronomy?), but it is important for students to understand how your scholarly training informs your teaching and to see that you have training that is separate and apart from your own personal experiences. This idea will likely be new to them, but ultimately being clear about your qualifications should add to your credibility. It is important to point out as well that this is much more difficult for instructors of color. Teacher identity plays an important and large role in how students perceive us, and people of color are especially likely to be thought of us as having a "personal agenda" when it comes to talking about race (Crittle & Maddox, 2017). These biases make it especially important and necessary for instructors marginalized by race to make their qualifications known.

The obvious way to lay out these qualifications is to make them part of your first-day activities. Research has generally shown that the first day is important with respect to setting expectations and seeding motivation (McGinley & Jones, 2014), so having some activities that allow you to outline your qualifications while also communicating your expectations for the course may be a good way to start. As an example, I do this by first laying out a brief outline of my education, my research on race, and the courses I have taught on race. To reinforce this idea, I often refer back to my discipline throughout the course (e.g., "this social psychological research. . . as a social scientist. . ."), a practice that I hope will re-center the content and reduce the likelihood that my students will see the material as being "just the teacher's opinion."

After laying out my own qualifications, I also like to ask my students to share their own expertise. I do this because I want to communicate that I care about them and that I want to get to know them, but also because I want to take advantage of the psychological principle of affirmation. Before describing that research, it helps to have an example. I first began asking my students about their own expertise after a particularly memorable experience with a resistant student. Early on one semester, I had asked the class to read a short piece on slavery and its role in the construction of race. Social anthropologist Audrey Smedley (2007) wrote the piece and I use it because students typically find it both readable and illuminating in terms of how we got the categories of "Black" and "White." One student, however, explained to me that she had read it and had asked her friend to read it as well and that they both agreed it was wrong. Trying not to look surprised or to be snarky, I asked her if she had done a lot of work in history or anthropology. She had not, of course, but instead of leaving it there, I asked her about her own expertise. I knew she was majoring in dairy science and that she was already working nearly full-time at a dairy farm just outside of town (I live in Wisconsin). I explained to her that I would never come to her farm and presume to understand it immediately any more than I would expect her to have a good understanding of the history of race so early in the semester. In that moment, her demeanor with me changed pretty dramatically. I could see that she appreciated feeling known and she quickly agreed that she would not like it at all if I tried to tell her how to do her job. She knew she was good at her work and she seemed to realize the implications of our conversation, as simple as they might sound: that one can have expertise in a topic that others do not have and cannot have unless they do the work of learning. That student still had some difficulties over the course of the semester, but she was engaged in class and she stopped resisting the material outright as she had before. She became more open to the work of learning even when it was difficult to accept.

To be clear, I do not mean to imply that we can always just "pull rank" on our students and dismiss their criticisms. This was a somewhat unique situation in that the student was not only skeptical of that reading, but also of her own ability to do well. She had come to see me because she felt that everything I was teaching (at least up to that point) was wrong and she did not believe she could learn and do well. She was worried that she would need to drop the course. What I wanted to communicate was not that she should just shut up and accept others' expertise, but that to learn, she would need to avoid dismissing it out of hand. That she had to grant some leeway to the experts as a way to learn more.

We talked a lot about how she had learned to do her job at the dairy, how she did not just "get it" right away but instead had learned from her mentor and supervisor over time as she watched him doing the job and as she took on more and more of the responsibility for herself.

From a psychological perspective, what I did by noting this student's expertise was a self-affirmation. Recent research in affirmation theory helps us understand why this technique works and how we can use it to our advantage as instructors. According to the theory, we generally like to perceive ourselves positively and as competent individuals (Crichter & Dunning, 2014). When that view of competence or positivity is threatened, we get defensive and resistant as a way of restoring our feelings of self-integrity. If, however, we are able to affirm our identity by focusing on an area of competence or on an important self-related value, then we can generally remain more open. Broadly speaking, affirmations help us view ourselves more expansively, as larger than the small threats we might face in the form of things we do not know or weaknesses we have (see Cohen & Sherman, 2014, for a review). Affirmations help us to remember how we have overcome challenges in the past, giving us the confidence and space to take on new challenges in the present.

As another example, and to help you see how this might happen in your own life, consider how you might feel if a colleague contradicts your ideas in a meeting. Imagine that this colleague does so by bringing up research or new information that directly contradicts your ideas and suggests a totally different approach. If you are like most people (myself included), you will cling to your original idea and try to find reasons why the new work is wrong or limited. You might sputter and stammer a bit, flopping around for a response. But what would happen if that same colleague also immediately pointed out how right you were about something else, something you had suggested the year before that had worked really well. Your new idea is still being discredited, but you are also being affirmed for what you know and for your ability to be helpful. Suddenly you feel less threatened and the defenses can come down. You still might not love that new research (and may immediately vow to look it up later), but you will probably be less likely to dismiss it out of hand. Because you have been affirmed, you do not have to defend yourself as strongly and you can be more open to new ideas.

In the chapters ahead, I will suggest other ways to use affirmation as a way to help students feel more open to threatening and difficult information. Research on both misinformation (Lewandosky et al., 2012) and racial bias (Adams, Tormala, & O'Brien, 2006) has shown affirmations to be effective. For now, you might consider incorporating a first-day activity that asks students to write about and share an area in which they hold some expertise as a way to start the semester off with a feeling of self-affirmation. I have found this activity to be both fun and useful on the first day. It allows me to get to know my students while also communicating that I care about them as people. Furthermore, it pairs nicely with me describing my own expertise when it comes to race. Finally, and depending on the context, I can use my knowledge of each student's expertise, referencing it casually in feedback or in class discussions as a way to help them feel seen and thus stay open to new information.

___

Chapter 2

STRUGGLING STUDENTS: HOW AND WHY RESISTANCE HAPPENS

___

IN THE FALL OF 2013, Shannon Gibney, a full-time adjunct professor of English at Minneapolis Community and Technical College (MCTC) was the subject of a formal reprimand. Her offense? Talking about racism in a communications class. According to Professor Gibney, two White male students in the class interrupted her to ask why the subject was even part of the course. According to Gibney, one of the students said, "I don't get this . . . It's like people are trying to say that White men are always the villains, the bad guys . . ." (Flaherty, 2013, p. 1). After trying to explain that discussing racism and describing how it operates was not personal, that it was about institutional racism, the students remained unsatisfied and defensive according to Gibney. She eventually advised them that they could file a racial harassment claim, which they did. After an investigation, the university reprimanded her for violating their civil rights.

As part of a statement issued just after the incident occurred, MCTC stated: "We expect that faculty will have the professional skills to lead difficult conversations in their classrooms and will teach in a way that helps students understand issues, even when students feel uncomfortable or disagree with particular ideas" (Flaherty, 2013, p. 3). But what are those skills? How do we work with students when they question our right to cover the material in the first place? Viewed through the lens of Shannon Gibney's experience, it is easy to see how instructors of race are so often put in impossible positions. When we teach what we know, we can be accused of "racial harassment" and reprimanded. Given outcomes such as this, it is easy to see why some instructors decide to avoid talking about racism in the classroom at all or become angry and forceful in their teaching. In this chapter I hope to help you work with resistance by describing and outlining how it works and providing some suggestions. I believe that if we can better understand resistance we can work more effectively with it.

To be clear, though, none of what I will cover here excuses incivility or disrespectful behavior. There are certainly times when no amount of understanding can ward off the angry denials of resistant students. I believe that Professor Gibney was unfairly treated by her institution and eventually they must have agreed, at least in part, because they rescinded her reprimand and removed it from her file, though it should be noted that this happened only after she went public and filed a grievance with her union (Williams & Gibney, 2014). In Shannon Gibney's case, her students went beyond the limits of acceptable classroom behavior and created a hostile environment. It is also no accident that Professor Gibney is a Black, female instructor. Studies have shown that instructors of color and women are especially likely to be on the receiving end of incivility, disrespectful behavior, and the questioning of their credentials (more on this in Chapter 3, see also Derald Wing Sue's 2015 book *Race Talk: The Conspiracy of Silence* for an overview of this issue and a general discussion of the silencing of most talk about race).

Given these limits, my intent in this chapter is to provide an overview of the most common forms of student resistance. While resistance can manifest in angry incivility as seen in the case above, most of the time it is more mundane and more manageable, and it can differ depending on the race of the student. By outlining the social psychological research that helps us to understand student resistance, I hope that you can better predict and prevent it within your own classroom. Using this research, as well as other studies of student resistance and incivility, I will also offer specific, evidence-based suggestions for minimizing resistance. My hope is to provide all of us who teach about race with some insights and some skills that we can use to maintain an effective learning environment.

WHAT IS RESISTANCE?

In her excellent edited book on teaching about privilege *Deconstructing Privilege* (2013), Kim Case, working with Elizabeth Cole, sets out to review the literature on student resistance and to provide additional evidence for "students' resistant behaviors in courses addressing privilege linked to social identities" (Case & Cole, 2013, p. 36). The authors offer readers a relatively concise definition, describing resistance as "the behavior of students who fail to engage with the course content, whether actively or passively" (Case & Cole, 2013, p. 34). Similarly, Stephen Brookfield in *The Skillful Teacher* (2015) describes resistance as "when students refuse to take seriously the learning you're pursuing." Both get at the same basic idea: you want students to learn but they are not engaging. This can happen in a variety of ways and for a variety of reasons, some of which I will try to outline here, but ultimately, in the words of Brookfield, "they have the right to resist." Looking at it from the students' perspective, resistance is all about reasserting some agency in a situation where the instructor holds most of the power. Moreover, when an instructor is teaching about race, students may feel especially "justified" in pushing back given that expertise in race is not something that most people accept in the same way that they might accept expertise in other academic areas. Putting these factors together, it makes sense that courses on race are spaces ripe for resistance.

Active and Passive Resistance

Resistance can come in different forms, ranging from challenging to upsetting to job threatening. We as instructors may hold a lot of power in our classrooms, but resistance in its most difficult forms can make that power feel small and our efforts to teach futile. On the active end of the resistance continuum are defensive or hostile comments in class, denial of the material presented, critical emails sent to the instructor (or department chair/dean), hostile nonverbal behavior, and grade challenges (Cho, 2011). These kinds of behaviors are more likely from those who feel empowered, typically White students and male students. Passive resistance, on the other hand, tends to involve withdrawal. Students avoid participation, engagement, and even eye contact in class. They may also stop attending, avoid reading assigned content, or prepare for class only superficially. This kind of behavior appears to be more likely for students of color (Case & Cole, 2013), but can also happen when students feel emotionally overwhelmed by the material. These students are not necessarily denying or rejecting class content outright, but their apathy looks like resistance all the same. For students of color in particular, what looks like resisting the material may actually be more about resisting the environment, particularly if the instructor is White and most of the students are White. I will say more about how resistance manifests differently for White students and students of color soon, but for now it is important to keep in mind that resistance can differ depending on the identity of the student and the larger context of the classroom.

Cognitive Simplification

In addition to the active and passive forms of resistance, another way to think about resistance is in terms of cognitive strategy. Frequently when I'm teaching about racism, I get some variation on what I call the "people suck" argument: "We are doomed to be racist because people are inherently bad" or "We are doomed to be racist because people are resistant to change, and it will take 100s (!) of years to improve." I began to think more deeply about these kinds of comments when I saw them popping up over and over again in a scholarship of teaching and learning project I completed with my colleagues Nancy Chick and Terri Karis. That study was a qualitative and quantitative assessment of four different classes centered on racism (each on a different campus and from a different disciplinary perspective). In it, we found that oversimplification and dualistic thinking were a common feature of the learning process. That is, students often seemed to jump to conclusions ("people are bad," "things won't change") as a way to shut down further reflection and avoid discomfort. As a result, and in the words of my co-authors, the students could feel a "self-satisfaction or self-confidence" that stopped them from having to dig deeper or learn further (Chick, Karis, & Kernahan, 2009, p. 9).

Another example of this kind of oversimplification comes not from my research, but from a conversation with a colleague. I note it here to show how this kind of thinking can come in unexpected ways and from students whom we might not ordinarily think of as resistant. A colleague who teaches about racism at a small, liberal arts college on the West Coast described to me the difficulties she was having with her students. Rather than denying the information about racism that she was presenting, the students instead pushed back at her for not being radical enough. They viewed her with suspicion for what they saw as her too measured and scholarly approach, pushing instead for stronger condemnations of racism and more certainty. According to my colleague, they were not necessarily wrong, but they also were not willing to think through the complexities and nuance inherent to the topic of race. Just as with the students described above, these students reached quickly for conclusions (i.e., racism is everywhere and equally horrible in all instances; racist people are bad and anti-racist people are good) as a way to avoid continued thought and reflection, and as a way to disengage from the difficulties and discomfort of learning.

WHY RESISTANCE HAPPENS?

Learning Is Not a Linear Process

One of the most basic building blocks of leaning, as we understand it, is that people add to existing knowledge to create new knowledge. In their important and essential book *How Learning Works*, Susan Ambrose and her colleagues argue that the nature of a student's prior knowledge plays an important role in how new information is assimilated. If that prior knowledge is inaccurate and consists of misconceptions, new learning can be particularly difficult and "resistant to correction" (Ambrose et al., 2010, p. 24). This happens because as we try to make sense of new information, we reconcile it with the old, thus creating hybrid models of knowledge that allow our misconceptions to continue. As an instructor, you have no doubt experienced the frustration of this, watching helplessly as students circle back to prior understandings in ways that you know are incorrect or simplistic.

With respect to race, the evidence is very clear that most prior learning is inaccurate or at least incomplete. As noted in Chapter 1, many Americans (especially Whites, but not only Whites) believe in the notion of colorblindness, rejecting the notion of widespread institutional discrimination. Similarly, there is little understanding of our history and the racist ideas that shaped the United States from the beginning (Kendi, 2016). Given this, it is not surprising that our students struggle to make sense of what we are teaching them and that they slip back just as we push forward. This has been noted by others who teach about race and have studied their students (Fallon, 2006), and we saw it as part of the larger study I described earlier (Chick et al., 2009).

Another way to think about this process is to view it through the lens of threshold concepts. You may recall Erin Winkler's work (described in Chapter 1) in which she conceptualized racism as a threshold concept—the sort of concept that is transformative and that students have to learn before they can learn other things (see Meyer & Land, 2005, for more on threshold concepts). Winkler (2018) showed that White students and students of color were able to cross the threshold, to learn and understand institutional racism as racism, but it took time and students of color learned more quickly than White students. William L. Smith and Ryan M. Crowley (2015) take a similar approach in their work with preservice teachers. They conceptualize race as a threshold concept and focus their work primarily on the process of oscillation. Oscillation is "a time in which the learner may regress and progress between states of understanding and acceptance" (p. 21). They write further that this process makes sense given that the learning of threshold concepts can involve shifts that are "personally disorienting" and that "one must renegotiate his or her identity within the parameters established by this new knowledge." In other words, learning about race involves seeing oneself in a new way and in a way that can be hard to "unsee." To glimpse this process, they closely analyzed the comments and contributions of one White student in particular as she learns about race in a course on social studies methodology. They document how she moves between statements of affirmation of what she is learning and denial "within seconds of each other" (p. 23). In concluding, they urge us as educators to understand this resistance and oscillation as part of the process and to slow down and use these oscillations as opportunities in the learning process rather than seeing them as simple avoidance.

But what does that look like? When I teach the psychology of prejudice and racism, I always begin with some American history. More specifically, I like to start with racial formation: the way that early Americans created the racial categories we have today as a way to justify their theft of labor (slavery) and land and all the discriminatory policies that made that theft possible. With respect to enslavement, I ask students to read a bit about how slavery enriched enslavers as well as other wealthy White Americans (e.g., those who traded in slave bonds, factory owners). We also cover how slavery benefitted all White Americans via the self-esteem and psychological benefits of White supremacy. That is, believing themselves to be White allowed White Americans to know that there was always another, lower class group below them no matter how poor they might be. Covering these ideas seems key in helping students understand how White supremacy works psychologically and why it continues to affect our thinking today.

In discussing slavery, there is not usually a lot of pushback from students. The historical nature of the topic seems to offer a comforting distance. Despite this, however, there is often a theme in the student comments that surprises me (though it should not): the idea that enslavement was wrong, but necessary to create the economically prosperous country we enjoy today as Americans. In one discussion, a White student asked me this question outright, "Without slavery would we be the prosperous country we are today? Wasn't it necessary, really?" The answer to this question is not straightforward and really comes down to "it depends." It depends on which Americans you mean when you say prosperous. Obviously, slavery did not enrich Black Americans. Furthermore, and according to historians, slavery really only enriched White people at the top of the economic ladder while giving modest economic benefits to Whites in the middle class and diminishing the economic prospects of poorer Whites even as they felt more superior through White supremacy (Baptist, 2014; Isenberg, 2016). These Whites were given a self-esteem boost perhaps, but not an economic one. Also, there were and are enormous costs to the system of White supremacy and racism that slavery created. These costs are economic, moral, and psychological, and they involve White people as well as people of color. Finally, we do not know what the United States would look like without slavery. It may have been more prosperous or prosperous in different ways. In discussing all of this, I have been lucky to have other students who could point out the unequal nature of the economic benefits of slavery and the costs that have accompanied them. It is also helpful to return to the evidence in the readings, the arguments and evidence of historians, again and again, to help students see the complexities of our messy history and reality.

What I think this example shows is how my students' prior knowledge of slavery was likely conflicting with what they were learning and how they were working to reconcile those differences. As James Loewen (2018) has pointed out in his book *Lies My Teacher Told Me*, most American students do not receive a clear picture of slavery in history class. Textbooks describe American slavery in very passive ways, as something that "just happened" rather than something actively pursued and defended to the point of war by rich White American landowners. The fuzzy and somewhat benign picture of slavery presented in American history textbooks is hard to square with a clearer vision of slavery linked directly to profit taking. I believe that for my students, as they are learning about racial formation, making slavery regrettable but inevitable is a way to reconcile previous knowledge (slavery just happened) with new knowledge (slavery was an actively pursued and heavily defended institution) to create a new understanding: The United States must have needed slavery to become the country we are today. In this reconciliation, we can also see another important psychological process that underlies student resistance and that we will cover next: the need to reduce feelings of cognitive dissonance.

Learning Can Arouse Justification and Rationalization

Few findings within social psychology are as robust and foundational as those that support cognitive dissonance theory. First identified by Leon Festinger, cognitive dissonance refers to the "state of tension that occurs whenever a person holds two cognitions (ideas, attitudes, beliefs, opinions) that are psychologically inconsistent" (Tavris and Aronson, 2015, p. 15). When we feel this tension, we are very motivated to reduce it, to rid ourselves of the mental discomfort that comes along with cognitive dissonance. An easy example of this for many of us is how we feel about work. Consider how you feel when you know you should be working, perhaps you have a manuscript to write or a stack of papers or tests to grade. At the same time, a walk with your daughter or your dog or even just yourself and your earbuds (my own favorite distraction) feels like a great idea. All of us get caught in such dilemmas regularly, and our minds are usually there to help supply us with a handy rationalization: "it's the first really nice day of spring" or "maybe my 14-year-old daughter will finally tell me what is bugging her, I can't miss that possibility" or "I can listen to this educational podcast." Whatever the reason, those justifications help to ease the tension we feel, allowing us to (mostly) enjoy our walk.

Now consider how this works when learning about race. When many students enter our classes, they are likely to believe that, at least for the most part, equality of opportunity (even if not in outcome) is a reality. After all, we have laws banning discrimination by race and we elected a Black president, right? Moreover, even if they see racism as a problem and recognize individual prejudice in those around them, they are still unlikely to recognize the broader realities of institutional racism. As our students learn, dissonance sets in. The scope and extent of racial bias will likely fuel a mounting tension between what they have always believed or been taught (society is a meritocracy where individual merit matters most) and the reality of what we are teaching them (racism is a pervasive feature, not a bug, of American life).

To reduce feelings of cognitive dissonance, all of us have to do one of two things: either change our existing beliefs or somehow discredit or alter the new information so that it cannot conflict with our prior understanding (Tavris & Aronson, 2015). As noted earlier, prior beliefs tend to be sticky. We like to return to them. When what we are learning causes cognitive dissonance, this process takes on an added complication. Not only do we have to reconcile prior information with new information, we also have a strong motivational need to do this in a way that resolves the tension we feel. We have to make both cognitive and emotional sense of what we are learning. In this situation, resistance becomes likely because resistance is a way to discredit or alter the new information so that it is not quite so upsetting. It is often easier to discredit the new information than to alter our existing beliefs.

To understand this better, it helps to understand just one more theory about human thinking. System justification theory explains that people "use ideas about groups and individuals to justify the way things are, so that existing social arrangements are perceived as legitimate, desirable, and fair" (Jost, 2011, p. 228). In other words, we want to believe that how things are is how they are supposed to be, that things are fair and right. The evidence for this theory suggests that our bias in favor of the status quo is quite strong. For example, we favor policies when we believe that they have been in place for a while as compared to policies we believe to be new (even if they are the same policy!) (Crandall, Eidelman, Skitka, & Morgan, 2009). If you think about it, you can see this bias in your own thinking or in those of your friends and colleagues. In my own academic department, I have watched new policies or programs that were once bitterly contested become normal or even championed by those who initially resisted them. The new policy becomes the status quo. When it comes to race, multiple social norms, institutions, policies, and implicit biases buttress our "existing social arrangements." The hierarchy we hold about race is deep and deeply ingrained in our minds as well as our environments. Seen this way, it is hardly surprising that challenging the racial status quo triggers justifications and rationalizations as well as resistance toward what we are teaching.

A final striking feature of system justification theory is the often-replicated finding that people may favor the status quo of social hierarchy even when doing so disadvantages their own social group. We like the status quo, even when the status quo does not really like us. The evidence in support of this is strong. Multiple studies have shown how those oppressed by racial or social hierarchy (African Americans, lesbians, and gay people) report bias in favor of those who are more advantaged (Whites, straight people). I mention this work and these findings specifically (see Jost, 2011, for a thorough review) as a way to help you better understand why it can be so difficult to teach about race, to deal honestly with something that is both deeply misunderstood and deeply disruptive to the status quo. As noted before, learning about race requires not only that students cognitively assimilate new information, but also that they emotionally assimilate it, moving past strong motives to justify the existing system of racial hierarchy. This process can be difficult for all students, regardless of race, but the resistance students exhibit will likely differ by race.

STUDENTS OF COLOR AND RESISTANCE

As a group, the needs and concerns of students of color are studied less than the needs and concerns of White students. This is particularly true when it comes to different racial groups within the "of color" umbrella. A few large-scale works have tracked the progress of multiple racial groups on campus (e.g., Sidanius, Levin, van Laar, & Sears, 2008), but these are relatively rare. Despite this lack of study, however, it is clear from the research that has been done that students of color, particularly Black and Hispanic students, are more likely to have experience with both racial discrimination and with discussions of race (Pew Research, 2016; Sue, 2015; Binder, 2014). These students also typically experience more interracial interaction compared to White students (Trawalter & Richeson, 2008). These prior experiences probably help when it comes to learning about race; recall Erin Winkler's (2018) findings about understanding racism and the greater speed with which Black students crossed the "threshold" of understanding about institutional racism as compared to their White peers. But this ease of learning can also translate into particular experiences of resistance.

Feeling Targeted and in the Spotlight

For many students of color, the classroom can be a place of feeling targeted by racism. Back in 1992, Beverly Daniel Tatum wrote about this as part of her study of how racial identity shapes learning. In describing how students of color can feel as they listen to their White counterparts, she quotes an African American student: "Sometimes I get real tired of hearing White people talk about the conditions of Black people. I think it's an important thing for them to talk about, but still I don't always like being around when they do it" (p. 206). She goes on to say that as the class has progressed, she is feeling less willing to listen and to be open to her White classmates' feelings and perspectives. Tatum describes this in terms of a heightened sensitivity, something she reports having seen often among her students of color, particularly as they listen to White students grappling with the realities of racism.

What is so striking to me about these findings is how similar they are to recent research. Case and Cole (2013) describe how students of color experience "target group resistance" by passively withdrawing from class activity. The authors argue that this happens because these students are seeking to avoid becoming representatives of their racial group (tokens) or to avoid being stereotyped or further marginalized. Just as for the student quoted above, these students know that the classroom could be unsafe for them and so it is more comfortable to skip class on certain days (depending on the topic) or to zone out during the discussion.

One other variable that is likely to make these feelings more likely: having a White instructor and/or predominantly White classmates. Research in social psychology on the spotlight effect has shown that when we are the sole representative of a salient social group, we are likely to feel more conspicuous and self-conscious. One particularly relevant set of experiments conducted by Jennifer Randall Crosby, Madeline King, and Kenneth Savitsky (2014) showed that when students of color were the sole representative of their race in a setting with other White students, the discussion of race caused them to feel not only more like they were the focus of others' attention but also to estimate that the

White people in the room were actually looking at them more frequently (as compared to a more neutral condition in which race was not being discussed). Most importantly, the students in this condition experienced much stronger negative emotions. Given these findings, it is not surprising that students of color might feel especially uncomfortable and likely to resist when they are surrounded by White people or hearing a White instructor talk about things with which they have such immediate and personal experience.

Feeling out of Control

In addition to feeling targeted, students marginalized by race are also likely to feel overwhelmed by the size and scope of racial bias. As we help students learn about racism in all its forms and effects, they will probably feel a tension not only between their prior understanding and their new learning, but also between what they believed about themselves and how they see themselves going forward. In addition to negative emotions like anger and sadness, there may also be a strong sense of powerlessness. We all like to feel in control of our lives, and the nature of racial bias makes that control more precarious for people of color. I have seen these feelings of distress in many of my own students. I vividly remember a Hmong American female student who was also very overweight saying to me that she just did not know how she was going to avoid job discrimination in her life after college. We had been covering psychological and sociological data on job and pay discrimination resulting from a variety of social identity characteristics. In that moment, it was obvious how distressing the information was for her. Why wouldn't it be? It makes sense that, as our students learn, they might need to step back to protect their own feelings of self-control and autonomy. Understanding and accepting that students will feel powerless can help us become more sensitive to the challenges they face and help us recognize why students who are marginalized by race may sometimes want to avoid the topic, thus leading to the resistance as withdrawal documented by both Tatum (1992) and Case and Cole (2013). In that moment with my student, I simply tried to listen and to accept her comments without brushing them aside or reassuring her.

Feeling Angry

It is important to note that students of color are also likely to feel angry as they learn more about racism. This is as it should be. Racism is life-threatening for people of color and it clearly shortens lives and decreases quality of life. As students learn about the extent of racism, they are also grappling with the very visible and well publicized instances of racism that we all see in the headlines and that can range from annoying to life-altering to life-ending. Putting all of this together is frustrating and often the root of anger. Again, this is normal and to be expected. The problem for our students, however, is that it is not acceptable to be emotional in class and anger can be especially taboo, particularly for Black students who may be stereotyped as angry even when they are not expressing anger. In discussing this kind of student anger, Stephen Brookfield, in a podcast interview with Bonni Stachowiak (2017), suggests that seeing models of other people of color who are feeling angry about racism and expressing that anger (perhaps in a video or audio interview, as part of a debate, etc.) could help students of color to feel that their anger is normal and to be expected. He also suggests being up front with students about these feelings of anger, naming them, and allowing time for reflection and writing on the part of students to help them process and grapple with their feelings of anger.

In general, it is important to keep in mind that students of color are likely to have a different and more difficult experience than White students. Because students of color typically have more experience with racism, they can often learn more quickly, as shown in the work of Erin Winkler (2018), whose Black students were quicker to grasp the concept of institutional racism. But the downside of this is that as a result of their more knowledgeable starting point, students of color sometimes gain less in terms of learning from diversity courses as compared to their White counterparts (Bowman, 2009). They are sometimes reviewing material that they already understand or patiently waiting as White students struggle to catch up. We also know that White people gain more as a result of cross-racial contact as compared to people of color experiencing that same contact, and this includes college students in interracial roommate situations (Sidanius et al., 2008; Tropp & Page-Gould, 2015). Here again the research tells us that students of color simply start from a stronger understanding of how racial bias works and have to work through the biases of the White people around them who are sometimes (though not always) learning and growing from those same encounters.

For all of these reasons, it is important to be sensitive to how students of color may be experiencing the classroom differently. As we will see below, White students can be much more vocal in their resistance, and their concerns can take attention away from the quieter experiences of our students of color, whose feelings may not be as obvious. Feelings of being targeted and in the spotlight, out of control, and angry in response to life-altering racism are important, and they are normal and rational responses. Later in this chapter and also in upcoming chapters, I will provide some specific, evidence-based suggestions for how to set up our courses in ways that may help to minimize the toll that learning about racism can take on our students of color.

WHITE STUDENTS AND RESISTANCE

In 2011 Robin DiAngelo coined the term "White fragility" and defined it this way: "a state in which even a minimal amount of racial stress becomes intolerable, triggering a range of defensive moves. These moves include the outward display of emotions such as anger, fear, and guilt, and behaviors such as argumentation, silence, and leaving the stress-inducing situation" (p. 54). DiAngelo deftly lays out the reasons for this fragility and the consequences of it, namely shutting down real and honest discussions of racism. From a teaching and learning perspective, the brittle nature of White people's reactions to learning about racism is one of the most potent drivers of resistance in our classrooms.

Am I Racist?

To understand White fragility, it helps to understand the personal implications of understanding racism for White people. As noted above, resistance via rationalization is a common response to learning about race. However, for White students (and White people more broadly), fear of being perceived as racist adds another driver to this rationalization process. Put simply, White people know that to be racist is to be "bad" and to be colorblind is to be "good." In general, and at the time of this writing, the norms of our society (mostly) do not condone open racial bigotry. Behaving in racist ways or expressing racial stereotypes that are not coded or cloaked in other more neutral terms is perceived as wrong.

As an example of how strongly White people can feel about being thought of as racist, consider the answer that former president George W. Bush gave to Matt Lauer in 2010 when asked about the worst moment of his presidency (Chappell, 2010). Despite large national tragedies such as the 9/11 terrorist attacks or the wars in Iraq and Afghanistan, Mr. Bush cited the moment when Kanye West described him as not caring about Black people in response to the aftermath of Hurricane Katrina. In the televised interview, Mr. Bush was visibly angry and upset, stating that West, "called me a racist." He goes on to say that he did not appreciate it and, when pressed, continued to insist it was the low point of his presidency. This despite numerous tragedies that occurred between 2001 and 2008. Put simply, being racist is a bad thing, particularly for White people. It conflicts with the desire of most people to see themselves positively, and for White people it is typically felt as a strong insult.

Returning to our students and to our definitions of racism, we can see that it is this shifting of racism from something that is easily avoided via behavior regulation (just be nice, do not openly discriminate) into something more institutional and systematic that creates the problem and the dilemma. If racism is a large and pervasive system, there is no easy way to escape or create personal distance. If I am White, I benefit. Period. This newfound understanding is upsetting and the implication that White students themselves are "racist" is a big part of what they are likely seeking to avoid through resistance.

But I Work Hard

Another, related and potent driver of resistance also derives from understanding racism as a system of advantage for White people. When asked if most people can get ahead if they work hard enough, a majority of Americans (61 percent) agree. According to Pew Research (2017) this strong support for hard work as a driver of success crosses all demographic and racial groups and has consistently been above average in American samples. As Wise and Case (2013) point out, this "myth of meritocracy" is a "psychological necessity" for privileged students (p. 19). Learning that racism is a larger system threatens to remove the sense of control that such beliefs in hard work can engender. We saw earlier how this loss of control can affect students of color. For White students, the myth of hard work is no less important and, in many ways, may be more important. Coming to understand that some of what you have is the result of unearned advantage feels unfair and conflicts strongly with the desire to see oneself positively and in line with larger American values of fairness and meritocracy.

Less Experience Than Other Students

White students are also much less likely to be experienced with discussions of race and racism as compared to their counterparts. In the survey of 14- to 24-year-olds conducted by MTV and published in 2014 (Binder), young White people were much less likely to say that they had been brought up in a household that discussed race (30 percent) as compared to young people of color (46 percent). This fits with other research showing how hesitant White parents can be to talk about race and racism with their children for fear of disrupting their "colorblind innocence" and how these norms carry into adult life (Vittrup, 2018). Many Whites simply avoid talking about race or racism at all because they believe that even mentioning race is a form of prejudice (Apfelbaum et al., 2008).

Importantly, White norms of avoiding all talk of race

affect everyone, including children of color. An interesting study published by Kristin Pauker, Evan P. Apfelbaum, and Brian Spitzer (2015) showed that in 9- to 12-year-olds, all students (White, Black, Asian, and Latino) avoided talking about race even when doing so would have substantially improved their performance on an experimental photo-identification task. If you know any 9- to 12-year-olds, or remember being one yourself, you will recognize how note-worthy this is: the kids in the study preferred to perform badly on a task in front of an adult (they were explicitly told that the goal was to perform well) rather than note the race of someone in a photograph. Results showed that the children's behavior was driven by their perceptions of the overall social appropriateness of mentioning race. That is, the more children believed that the adults in their lives did not like to talk about race then the more likely they were to follow those norms. The authors of this study concluded that it was White parents and teachers who were most strongly communicating to the children in this study that race talk is negative and to be avoided, thus enforcing colorblind norms for all of the children. For White students, then, the message of avoiding race talk is doubly reinforced, both at home and at school. These White children then become White college students, inexperienced and uncomfortable with talking about race and racism.

RECOMMENDATIONS AND SUGGESTIONS

Shannon Gibney, found guilty of racially discriminating against two White male students because she discussed structural racism in class, has continued to write about this incident and about the challenges inherent in teaching racism as a Black female professor (Williams & Gibney, 2014). Her writing is important, especially because resistance to what we teach is not decreasing. If anything, resistance may be increasing as more students go public with complaints about their professors and as professor comments are publicized and magnified across social media and in the blogosphere (regular readers of the *Chronicle of Higher Education* or *Inside Higher Ed* will know what I mean). I would never suggest that we, as instructors, can control or stop the resistance we face. This is especially true for faculty of color who are more vulnerable to the most potent and toxic forms of resistance. There are, however, things we can do to try to remain in control of our classrooms and ensure the best possible chance for learning. Indeed, much of the rest of this book is focused on creating a positive teaching environment for you and for your students. To start, I want to note one specific idea, with different variations, that I believe fits nicely with the explanations I have just provided for why resistance happens.

Allowing and Affirming Marginalized Identities

If you teach about race, it is very likely that at some point in your teaching you have heard, often from a White student, some variation on the following: "But I am a woman/poor person/gay person/rural person/inner-city person/etc., I experience discrimination because of that and so I cannot be racist." In talking with other people who teach about race, I have heard this a lot and certainly experience it myself. It is quite common for White students to focus in on some other marginalized identity (social class, gender, sexual identity, religion) when learning about racism. In my own experience, this is particularly likely when structural or institutional racism are the topics of consideration. The implications of a deeply unjust system based on skin color are cognitively and emotionally difficult to assimilate. One escape hatch that can provide relief is claiming hardships of one's own. "How can I be privileged if I have had all these other challenges to deal with? I am not really a part of this system." Indeed, recent research has shown that when White people read a simple one-paragraph description of White racial advantage they became more likely to claim greater life hardships and setbacks in a subsequent survey (Phillips & Lowery, 2015). Further exploration of these findings showed that these participants did not necessarily deny the existence of White privilege overall, they just wanted to be clear that this advantage did not extend to them. In other words, they were using greater personal hardship as a way to exempt themselves, personally, from the advantages of White supremacy and institutionalized racism.

So, what to do? How to work with this need to distance? Ironically enough, the way out might be through. In other words, accepting students need to claim hardship and perhaps even helping them see it for themselves. To clarify, consider the findings of Ashley Shelby Rosette and Leigh Plunkett Tost (2013). These researchers ran a series of experiments examining how thinking about identity might influence privilege recognition. What they found was that when White women or Black men were aware of the ways in which they had likely been disadvantaged by their sex or race respectively, they were then more likely to recognize their privileges along the other dimension of their identity (race or sex, respectively). Careful analysis showed that their privilege recognition was mediated by their perceptions of their own group's disadvantage. In other words, the perception of disadvantage for their own group came first, followed by subsequent privilege recognition for the other, more advantaged, part of their identity (race for the White women, sex for the Black men).

These laboratory-based findings fit nicely with the writing of Wise and Case in their writing about privilege resistance (2013). In describing how they work with resistant students, Wise and Case emphasize the importance of intersectionality or focusing on how a variety of "privileged and oppressed social identities interact simultaneously within each individual" (p. 23). Recognizing and claiming their own disadvantage via less privileged identities, they argue, seems to validate and affirm the students. Once this occurs, people can open up and begin to recognize the privileged identities they hold as well as the disadvantage that others hold. Reading this, two things jumped out at me. First, helping students understand and think about their own marginalized identities has often worked well for me too. I typically ask students, within the first weeks of class, to think about and reflect on their own various social identities and the privileges that accompany them (I provide a list of several possible categories). They write down some thoughts and experiences, discuss those within small groups, and then we move into whole class discussion. Just as Wise and Case recommend, I try to ensure that everyone can think about at least one relatively high-privilege group to which they belong (e.g., college student, thin person, being White, being heterosexual) and one relatively low-privilege group to which they belong (e.g., being Black, LGBTQ). Not all groups are equal, of course, but considering a wide variety of social groups sets up a variety of important concepts that I hope to teach around the importance of context, relative social power, and intersectionality.

A second insight, and perhaps more important, is why this kind of technique might reduce resistance. For this, we have to delve a bit into the psychology of self-affirmation that I noted at the end of Chapter 1 (see Cohen & Sherman, 2014, for a lengthy review of self-affirmation). As you may recall, when we feel a threat to our sense of self, to the notion that we are generally good or correct, most of us constrict our view. We focus primarily on the threat. Self-affirmation in the face of threat helps us to widen our attention back out so that we can see the bigger picture. Research shows that this process can lead to change and personal growth as people engage more with their weaknesses and mistakes and stop their defensive reactions and denial. As just one example, studies have shown that people are more open to threatening health information (e.g., smokers reading about how smoking can lead to lung cancer) when they have experienced a self-affirmation (Cohen & Sherman, 2014). Affirmation mitigates the natural tendency to shut down and constrict our view when faced with threatening information, thus allowing us to engage with new information and see things in new ways.

Obviously, learning about racism can be threatening. Affirmations of our students' sense of self should help them to broaden their thinking beyond that threat. Returning to the suggestion of Wise and Case (2013) and the way in which I ask my students to consider their own social identities, I would argue that doing this is an affirmation of the self. When students reflect on various parts of themselves, when they describe their experiences with respect to their own social identities and have those experiences validated by other students and by me as the instructor via discussion, this is affirming. As a result, the *threat* of learning about racial privilege, especially for White students, may literally take up less attentional space, providing students with the room to engage more with the *idea* of privilege. Furthermore, a self-affirmation coming early in the semester (first week or so), has the potential to shape how White students perceive all the content that comes afterward, setting up a cycle of affirmation and engagement that can reinforce itself over time, ultimately leading to greater learning.

Just to be clear that self-affirmation can work in the context of race and privilege, it is important to remember that the study cited earlier (Phillips & Lowery, 2015) is one of several to show that when White participants are affirmed, they are less likely to defensively deny information about White privilege or institutional racism. In that particular study, White people who completed a quick self-affirmation were then less likely to claim their own hardship in reaction to reading a one-paragraph description of White privilege. Taken together, the research on self-affirmation suggests that providing self-affirmations to students may be akin to a kind of inoculation we can give to our students to help them learn and to help our classrooms run a bit more smoothly.

When it comes to students of color, there is one more affirmation that I believe is important. Given the benefits described above, I think all students can learn more after they are given the chance to feel affirmed in their various social identities. However, students of color also need the affirmation that comes from having their own previous experiences with racism affirmed as well. As noted at several points above, students of color have life experiences that can give them an edge in understanding and learning, but that can also make them feel targeted and in the spotlight, particularly with a White instructor and/or predominantly White classmates. For these reasons, it is important to let students of color know that we as instructors, especially if we are White, understand that they have important previous experiences with racism that we may not have. We can let them know that we understand that these experiences are personal, important, and unique to them even as we hope that they will learn more. Sending an email early in the semester or having a short out-of-class conversation about this can be affirming for students of color and help them to feel more open as the class continues. You could also use that conversation as a way to let them know, particularly if they are one of the only students of color in the classroom, that you do not expect them to be the representative for their race and that sharing their experiences is up to them.

Recently, after covering racism and prejudice in my social psychology course (a course that touches on these topics but that covers many other topics as well), I had a conversation with a student that I believe illustrates how such affirmations can increase the interest and openness of students of color. Beginning in class and extending into my office hours afterward, this student told me about how her experiences in high school had taught her to try and be more thoughtful about race. As a biracial student who identified as Latina but who had a White parent, she saw herself as someone who could see "all sides" as she put it. As we talked, it became apparent to me that while she had a lot of experience both hearing and being the target of stereotypes and bias she was also missing a broader understanding about how racism works institutionally and culturally. We talked for a long time. As we did, I tried to listen closely to her stories and to emphasize that with her experiences she really had an advantage over many of her predominantly White classmates, most of whom have not had diverse or integrated schooling experiences and most of whom have not witnessed racial bias in real or personal ways. I also told her that I thought she should try to push herself to learn more about how racism and discrimination work as a way to supplement those experiences and help her talk to others around her about racism and discrimination (something she said she wanted to do). I urged her to consider taking my course on prejudice and racism the next semester. Several days later she approached me again and we talked some more. After several of these conversations, she told me that she was indeed planning to enroll in the course and was looking forward to it. She has never told me this directly, but I got the feeling that she had not been planning to take my course on prejudice and racism until after we talked (it is an elective in the psychology major, but not required). I think I had to show her that I respected her experiences and that I could listen in addition to teaching.

—

Chapter 3

GETTING YOURSELF TOGETHER: DEVELOPING A SECURE TEACHER IDENTITY

—

IN 2015, Dr. Chenjerai Kumanyika, a professor of communications at Rutgers University who teaches regularly about race and racism, described his experience attending a vigil for the victims of that year's Emanuel AME Church shooting by a White supremacist. All of the victims were Black and were murdered because they were Black. In the post, published on NPR's *Code Switch* blog (2015), Kumanyika describes how difficult it is to simultaneously cope with being the victim of racist suspicion while at the same time appeasing and comforting the White people who are suspicious. The example he gives concerns a White police officer he encountered before the vigil, but in the essay, he likens it to teaching:

Today, it means that when I discuss these shootings with my white students and my heart is bursting with outrage and grief, I must keep my voice and gestures gentle and calm and validate

my students' most hurtful comments so they don't feel person-
ally indicted.

What is so striking about that comment is how similar it
is to other comments I have heard from fellow teachers of
race and how it exemplifies some of the advice I first read
when I began teaching about the psychology of racism nearly
20 years ago. At the time, I was lucky enough to discover the
incredibly thorough and important guidebook *Teaching for
Diversity and Social Justice* (now in its third edition, 2016).
The authors advised then, and still do, that instructors be
aware of and prepared for the challenges we will face in the
classroom. Specifically, we have to understand how the comments of our students will be upsetting and how we will have
to work out our own feelings well before we are interacting
with students in the classroom. They advise that to do this
kind of work you have to be able to let the class be about
the participants and not about you or your experiences and
feelings. In his teaching, Kumanyika was doing just that,
letting go of his own feelings as a way to make space for
the learning of his students. This is not easy though. It is
emotionally difficult to suppress your own very valid and
natural reactions so that someone else's feelings can take
precedence.

Several years ago, I was talking to another instructor, a
Black woman from another university, who described how
she could feel her blood pressure rise as she read the comments of her students (she teaches African American studies
and literature). She told me at the time that her boyfriend
felt it was unhealthy for her to teach what she did, that it
might not be worth it for her to teach such content given
the stress of reading student comments that were clueless at
best and seriously resistant at worst. I have wondered about

this myself, noting the feelings of anger and sadness rising as I grade posts before class and try to work out how best to respond to ideas that are factually inaccurate or insensitive. Moving through those feelings to a place where I can use their comments for the purposes of learning is not easy. Ultimately, I know that the benefits outweigh the costs. I also know that this is much, much easier for me to do as a White person than it is for my colleagues of color.

In this chapter, we will cover some of the difficulties inherent in teaching about race from the point of view of the instructor. The lower teaching evaluations, the emotional difficulty, and the ways in which these consequences differ depending on race, gender, academic status, and the corporatization of the university. After looking at these problems, we will then focus on solutions. What instructors can do for themselves and for each other to make the work a little easier and, hopefully, more enjoyable. If you are reading this, you likely care a great deal about your teaching and your students' learning. It should be challenging work, for sure, but it should still be doable and not be so upsetting that it pushes you into angry self-righteousness or resignation and withdrawal.

TEACHING EVALUATIONS AND TEACHING ABOUT RACE

For those who teach about race, it is a truism that your evaluations can suffer. In my own experience, I often receive bi-modal or polarized evaluations. Some students love the class and the content, gushing that everyone should be required to learn about race while a few others feel stifled and singled out. These are the ones I remember the best, of course, even though at most the negative comments usually only come from two or three students. One recent example from this category was a student who complained in the written section of the evaluations that I should use more Fox News as a way to balance out my overly liberal perspective. This same student went on to say that they felt as if they had been unable to speak in class, unable to express viewpoints in disagreement with the dominant perspective. This bothered me, of course, and made me vow to continue working on the classroom climate, creating a space that is open, welcoming, and conducive to community. But it also struck me that I rarely get this kind of comment in the other courses I have taught. I cannot remember ever receiving a challenge to my sources when teaching social psychology or a course on careers in psychology. Not one student has ever said I need more from "the other side" or that I need to provide content that contradicts the studies and research I have presented. I know that I am not alone in this; many others have written about how their evaluations suffer and about the backlash they receive when they teach about race (Cho, 2011). Some research bears this out: Boatright-Horowitz and Soeung (2009) found that evaluations were indeed lower for instructors teaching about White privilege as compared to those teaching a lesson on social learning theory.

In understanding these lowered teaching evaluations, it is important to keep in mind the race of the instructor. I have sometimes had people ask if I (as a White woman) have a more difficult time teaching about race because I am White and am presumed to have had less personal experience with discrimination. They wonder if I am challenged more around questions of expertise. While I can understand this assumption, this has not been my experience. As noted at the start of the chapter, I do find it difficult to teach about race and have seen my share of negative evaluations as a result, but I do not believe that my race has added to this difficulty.

My experience, however, is one of someone who teaches predominantly White students. It may be worth examining how other White instructors who teach more students of color experience teaching about race. Unfortunately, as of this writing, I have been unable to find research on this particular question. Instead, what is clear is that people of color receive lower teaching evaluations overall as compared to White instructors (Bavishi, Madera, & Hebl, 2010), a pattern that is likely worsened when the topic is race.

Consider some of the conclusions of a review article written by Crittle and Maddox (2017). Drawing on research from several areas of social psychology, the authors show that those who are the victims of discrimination (e.g., women, people of color) are viewed as complainers when they draw attention to problems of discrimination (importantly, women receive lower teaching evaluations on average even when the topic is not race; see MacNell, Driscoll, & Hunt, 2015, for one example). What this means is that even though these groups have more direct and personal experience with discrimination, discussing that experience or the racism that underlies such experiences is seen as illegitimate when compared to the same message coming from a White person. Crittle and Maddox conclude that instructors of color and especially women of color may be viewed as less professional and less objective when compared to their White counterparts. Along those lines, research has shown that instructors of color often have their credentials questioned by students (Sue, Rivera, Watkins, Kim, Kim, & Williams, 2011). Seeing this, it becomes obvious that teaching about race is more difficult for those who are not White and especially for women of color.

A recent study, conducted and published by psychologists interested in how this greater toll on faculty of color might be

affecting the field of counseling psychology, confirmed a lot
of what earlier research has shown and pointed toward some
additional concerns. Ahluwalia, Ayala, Locke, and Nadrich
(in press) conducted in-depth interviews with 12 faculty of
color who teach Multicultural Competence (a required course
for all graduate-level counseling students) and uncovered
multiple themes illustrating the difficulties of teaching this
course. First, faculty of color are often expected to teach
this course (along with those who are junior in status or
adjunct) while White faculty are not. The authors note that
this is part of a larger pattern throughout academia: that
women and faculty of color are the ones teaching about race
or including racial content in other courses, increasing their
chances of receiving negative evaluations. They also found
that these faculty were challenged by the need to juggle multiple goals as they taught: staying open in the face of hateful
or resistant comments, moving the class as a whole toward
greater learning even in the face of resistance, and ensuring
that individual students did not feel marginalized (particularly students of color). Such experiences took a toll, with
most of the participants noting the emotionally draining
nature of the work and the ways in which their other work
(scholarship especially) suffered as a result of the increased
use of energy that teaching about race often entails. At the
same time, many also noted how fulfilling and rewarding
such teaching can be, even in the face of these difficulties
(though at least one participant noted that they no longer
want to teach the course because the costs had begun to feel
greater than the rewards). Finally, most of the instructors
spoke about the negative impact of this teaching on their
evaluations and the need for department chairs, colleagues,
and deans to understand how the content of such courses
can affect evaluations.

"But Hurt Feelings Can Be Bad for Business"

In 2013, the sociologist and public intellectual Tressie McMillan Cottom wrote the words above as part of a piece exploring how the "customer service" model of education contributes to the difficulties in teaching about race. In this piece, she was responding specifically to the Shannon Gibney case. In that case, Gibney was reprimanded by her college for the "racial harassment" of White male students in her communications class when they objected to her teaching about institutional racism. As noted previously, Gibney's reprimand was rescinded after the college completed an investigation and Gibney continues to teach at the same college, but the investigation took nearly a year to complete and Professor Gibney received national scrutiny as a result of the incident.

After describing Gibney's experience, Cottom goes on to make several important observations about the teaching of race in a time of declining state support. As colleges and universities become more tuition dependent, a new emphasis on students as customers has developed and instructors are caught in the middle. While universities want to make their students (and those students' parents) happy, instructors know that students also deserve meaningful learning outcomes. Achieving those outcomes, however, may mean that students, and especially White students, will have hurt feelings as they begin to understand the institutional nature of racism, the extent of White supremacy and privilege, and the ways in which they themselves have both benefitted from and been diminished by this larger system.

Complicating all of this further is the precarious nature of academic employment. As noted in the Introduction, I myself am mostly insulated from the uncertainties of our current job market. I am a tenured full professor in a discipline that has consistently had strong enrollment (psychology). The new norm in academia, though, is not for the kind of job that I hold. Nearly 70 percent of those who work in academia, according to the American Association of University Professors, are contingent, adjunct, non-tenure-track faculty (as cited in Baker, 2016). For these instructors, pleasing your customers can become paramount. If you are working on a semester-to-semester basis, anything you do to upset your students, create strife, and, perhaps worst of all, disrupt the harmony that department chairs, deans, provosts, and other administrators are working to maintain is likely to result in your not being renewed or in damaging your reputation as an instructor.

In putting all of these factors together, it is impossible not to double down on the point that the burden of these trends falls more heavily on people of color and especially women of color. Overall, women are more likely to be represented in the ranks of adjunct instructors and women of color are especially likely to hold such positions (Gonzalez & Harris, 2012). As a result, lower teaching evaluations and the questioning of credentials that are already more likely for these groups will have an outsized effect on the work and careers of some instructors as compared to others. Chandra D. L. Waring and Samit Dipon Bordoloi (2013) write about the difficulties of this intersection in an article they titled " 'Hopping on the Tips of a Trident': Two Graduate Students of Color Reflect on Teaching Critical Content at Predominantly White Institutions." In the article, they reflect on three different but intersecting challenges in their work: "teaching critical content [about power and privilege], being minorities, and being graduate instructors" (p. 104). They write eloquently about the difficulties inherent in teaching with respect to each of these identities, but it is in their combined influence where it becomes easy to see how the context of a particular class can really influence the experiences and well-being of an instructor. As just one example, Waring describes how at one point she began to dread going to class despite a love for teaching. An older, White, male student was regularly questioning her teaching and she knew that this would be less likely had she not been a (young) graduate instructor, a woman of color, and if the class had not been so focused on power and privilege. The confluence of these factors allowed this particular student to feel comfortable in his resistance to learning. He told Waring that his years of experience were enough to see that what she was teaching was wrong and that he understood things far better than she, the instructor, possibly could!

What this means for those of us who teach about race is that we need to consider the full context of our teaching as a way to understand the unique difficulties we face. In my teaching, I often ask students to think of themselves as a collection of social identities. Some of those identities may offer protection or privilege (being White or male or heterosexual) and some will confer disadvantage (being a person of color or being fat). These identities interact with every situation we find ourselves in to create the advantage or disadvantage we experience. As instructors, who we are (race, gender, age, size) will interact with the hierarchy and power structure around us to help determine our experience. Keeping our own identities and context in mind can help us better understand the difficulties we face and stop us from internalizing our negative experiences in the classroom. What we do is hard and the context in which we do it can make it harder. So, what can we do to better understand and perhaps even improve our experiences? How can we use what we know to get around our students' resistance without compromising our effectiveness or our well-being? I will begin with suggestions at the individual level and move towards more institutional and systemic solutions.

RECOMMENDATIONS AND SUGGESTIONS

Know the Content

In 2013, Pasque, Chesler, Charbeneau, and Carlson published a study reporting the results of their interviews with over 65 faculty about racial conflict in the classroom. They identified a number of themes in the answers of their racially diverse and mixed-gender sample, ranging from avoidance of race to deliberate attempts to introduce racial conflict into their classrooms. In discussing their findings, they noted the difficulty that most instructors experience when it came to race in the classroom and they argued that faculty need to have better tools with which to do this work, including a strong knowledge base with respect to how students learn, how classroom dynamics work, and about race and racism overall.

Being comfortable and confident in our teaching can be, at a basic level, about our knowledge base. Subject matter knowledge is typically one of the first questions included in standard student evaluations of teaching. We know we will be judged. Standing in front of a class, we also know how scary it is to field questions that we cannot answer. Most of us learn to "tap dance" as a friend of mine calls it, but it is usually better to feel that we really know our subject inside and out. The more we know, the more confident we can feel as we answer questions and deal with content challenges.

In teaching the psychology of prejudice and racism, I have found that the content I have most needed and wanted to learn more about is the history of race and White supremacy in the United States. I am a social psychologist, not a historian, but I have gravitated toward learning about history as a way to improve my courses and put the psychological concepts we cover into broader context. I have come to believe that it is impossible to talk about race in any meaningful way without first defining it and understanding how it came to be within a specific national context. Luckily, there are a number of excellent and accessible sources written by historians for general audiences: *Lies My Teacher Told Me* by James Loewen, *The Half Has Never Been Told* by Edward Baptist, and *Stamped from the Beginning* by Ibram Kendi, to name just a few (see the Appendix for a complete listing). There are also excellent documentaries, podcasts, and interviews that include expert historians we can learn from. Early on in my teaching career, I set a goal for myself to read at least one book about American racial history every year, usually in the summer (I also regularly consume other research, media, and books about race of course). I do not typically assign most of what I read to my students (how could I!), but that is not the point. Learning more is about me, and I have found that doing this accomplishes several goals at once. First, it helps me model continued learning for my students. I often bring the books I have read or am reading to class and I create a "resource list" each year of other media and books, helping them to see that no expert ever "knows it all" and that part of expertise is continual learning and growth. Second, the more I learn the better I am at fielding questions and challenges as they arise. Finally, and perhaps more importantly, the more I learn the more confident and comfortable I feel while teaching. History may not be the particular area you choose to learn more about (particularly if you are already a historian!), but there are multiple disciplines to choose from (history, literature, sociology, psychology, economics, etc.) or you may choose to move around, learning from a variety of perspectives. Whatever you do, learning more is likely to help you feel more confident in your teaching and better able to see your students' learning in a larger context.

Know Yourself

Aside from knowing our stuff, we also need to know ourselves. How are we advantaged or disadvantaged by race? How do our other social identities (gender, social class, religion, etc.) affect us and shape how we see ourselves? What biases do we carry and when have we acted on them? These questions are important to ask and critical to our ability to understand ourselves as we teach about race. If we are asking our students to learn about the system of racism and to see how they themselves fit into that system, we have to do that work as well. Grappling with this difficulty is necessary for learning and part of how we can all begin to see beyond just our own personal experiences when it comes to race. As we understand how we ourselves are part of a larger system of racism and White supremacy, we can see the ways that other people fit too and why their experiences are likely to be different from ours.

As a White person, I have tried to be very concrete with myself about how my race has influenced my life. It is not comfortable, but I need to be honest about how my advantages have shaped me and how I continue to benefit from being White. Doing this helps to keep me humble in the face of what I am teaching and enables my ability to see that I am not exempt from racism or White supremacy simply because I understand how it works. Several years ago, I won a prestigious statewide diversity award, something that was both honoring and surprising. Since that time, however, I have noticed that this particular award is often given to White people. To be fair, the state I live and work in is very White and less diverse than most states in the country. But I also know that there are a lot of people working within my university system who are very deserving and who have not won this award despite doing work very similar to my own. I believe they deserve the award just as much or more than I do and I cannot help but note that these people are people of color, including women of color. This is just one example, but it illustrates how race has worked to benefit me, even with respect to something that is supposed to be about people of color.

As another example, Samit Dipon Bordoloi (one of the graduate instructors cited above, Waring & Bordoloi, 2013) describes how understanding his own multilayered social identity has been important for his teaching. As a "middle-class, upper-caste Indian" man, Bordoloi experienced quite a change when he moved to the United States for graduate work. He notes that until he arrived and began to experience marginalization at the hands of his White teachers and classmates, he had never really experienced much bias. The anger he felt became confrontational, but he states that he "quickly realized . . . that such an attitude would not be helpful while teaching a predominantly White student population" (p. 112). Instead, he tried to think more critically about his own blindness to male and class privilege, how he had always minimized the role of such advantages in his own success. He realized that to help others learn about their racial advantage, he would need to acknowledge his own advantages. For Bordoloi, the experiences of marginalization and privilege were important for his own self-understanding and provided ways for him to connect with his students.

Understanding that racism benefits me or that sexism

benefits Samit Bordoloi is not about self-flagellation and it is not always necessary to share these kinds of experiences or insights in class (more on that in a minute). Instead, what I am urging is that you engage in the same process you are asking your students to engage in: thinking about how racism works as a system without either exempting your own experiences or focusing excessively on them as a way to resist learning.

To be clear, we do not always need to share our thoughts about ourselves or our experiences with our students. Just because I understand that racism benefits me does not mean that I am required to openly disclose these feelings to a class, particularly if I am modeling unproductive, excessive guilt or if I come off as overly self-deprecating. On the flip side, sharing experiences of disadvantage can also create problems. As we have seen, instructors of color are especially at risk of looking as though they are simply teaching from a personal agenda, making them vulnerable to resistance (Crittle & Maddox, 2017). If you have been marginalized by race and experienced racial discrimination, sharing those experiences can be risky as well. The skill to cultivate appears to be one of first knowing ourselves and working out, before we teach, how our experiences reflect the larger forces we are trying to teach about. When we are secure in our self-knowledge, we should be able to use our experiences thoughtfully and strategically, being open and vulnerable where needed to help students connect, modeling thoughtful learning, but also letting the class be about the students rather than about ourselves.

Know Your Own Power

As Sarah Cavanagh notes in her book about emotion in the classroom (2016), instructors have a lot of power. For the most part, we are the ones who decide on the content, set up the assignments, and determine grades. As Cavanagh puts it, we "restrict students' freedom" in the ways we command their attention, through the work we assign, and in the standards we set (p. 191). She goes on to note how this differential in power sets up many potential power struggles and the possibility for negative emotion and discord in the classroom. To avoid this, she recommends trying to use our power more wisely and without coercion or authoritarianism ("because I say so").

An example of this can be found in the writing of Waring and Bordoloi (2013). Both authors describe getting clear about the power they held as they were beginning to teach and how they could use their power to more effectively teach about racism and privilege. For example, Bordoloi found that his discussion guidelines were essential to feeling effective as an instructor. He writes about how trying to assert his legitimacy through his credentials (his multiple degrees) really did not work. It felt superficial. But demonstrating his authority via clear rules and classroom structures greatly improved his experience in the classroom. His co-author describes a similar feeling as she realized that her main power in teaching was in setting up the assessments. By carefully designing papers that required particular types of knowledge and evidence, she could feel more confident that her goals were driving her assessments and that her students were moving towards the kinds of learning she wanted them to have. Each of these instructors did the work of thinking carefully about what they wanted for their students and how they could use their power to carry out those goals.

I recommend trying to follow a similar process. Getting some clarity around the power you hold and how you can use it effectively can be a way to avoid petty power struggles and help you to feel more in control. To do this, you can think through your specific course objectives (what do you most want your students to learn) and then tie them into your policies, assignments, and assessments. It can also be helpful to remember what you can and cannot control. I accept that I cannot really compel my students to change their attitudes or behavior. It is not my job to coerce them into a particular way of thinking, but I can help them see how prejudice and racism work psychologically and hold them accountable for that understanding in their written discussion comments and papers. I can require that they use evidence and disallow it or challenge them when they make claims that have no support and that deny the reality of what I am teaching. Finally, I can be clear and transparent in doing all of this so that they can see how I am using my power and how it relates back to my discipline rather than to my own personal beliefs or agenda (clear grading rubrics, clear assignments, and a clear syllabus). I may still receive pushback, especially if I am young, contingent in status, a woman, and/or a person of color, but the research suggests that the more I can be transparent about my goals and rationale, the better off I will be.

Increase Your Personal Resources

A 2011 study published by Sue, Rivera, Watkins, Kim, Kim, and Williams reported the findings of interviews with eight experienced instructors, all people of color, who were not necessarily teaching courses on race but who had all experienced racial conflict in the classroom. The interviews and analysis revealed a number of interesting findings, but one theme that really jumped out at me concerned the instructors' feelings of internal struggle. Participants described juggling a number of disparate thoughts at once including:

1) how to balance appearing objective and neutral while also supporting their students, 2) dealing with microaggressions directed at them by students, 3) knowing that they are likely to be perceived as experts on race simply because of their own race, 4) knowing that they are expected to be good at managing discussions on race simply because of their own race, and 5) managing their own personal thoughts and feelings. It is exhausting just to read!

Similarly, and more recently, Ahluwalia et al. (in press) found that most of the 12 instructors of color they interviewed, all teaching Multicultural Competence in Counseling, described a similar dynamic. They reported facing multiple and competing issues as they taught: staying open in the face of hateful comments, moving the class forward in terms of learning goals, and protecting individual students from marginalization. As a White instructor, I obviously have fewer of these challenges. I am not subjected to microaggressions based on race, for example. But I do face the challenge of staying open in the face of hateful and resistant comments, and I often find it challenging to juggle the competing and cascading thoughts and feelings that are present when teaching about race (e.g., guiding the discussion, protecting marginalized students, connecting student comments to each other and to the larger learning goals). Luckily, there are some evidence-based ways to potentially manage this challenge.

Within the first several years of teaching, I became interested in mindfulness and meditation for reasons that were (mostly) unrelated to my work. I started practicing in an informal way and without any training outside of my own reading. Just like a lot of other folks, I found the experience of meditation both frustrating and illuminating. What surprised me, though, was how it changed my experience of the classroom. This was not something I had expected at all, but it is something I have since heard from a variety of other instructors who began a meditation practice after they had started teaching. I was not radically different as I was teaching, but I was different, especially in facilitating discussion. I began to feel a stronger sense of control and a better ability to work with frustrating student comments and complex classroom situations. Since that time, I have read a lot more about the science of mindfulness and discovered the work of contemplative pedagogy (the application of contemplative practices, including mindfulness, to teaching and learning; see Barbezat & Bush, 2014, for an introduction). Since learning more, especially about the science of mindfulness, it seems clear that this practice could be very helpful for those teaching emotionally provocative content, including race.

There is a lot of literature on the science of mindfulness, so I will focus on a few main findings from the review article published in 2011 by Hölzel, Lazar, Gard, Schuman-Olivier, Vago, and Ott. In the article the authors lay out the mechanisms through which mindfulness meditation works and they begin with the most common definition for mindfulness: "nonjudgmental attention to experiences in the present moment" (p. 538). They go on to clarify that most researchers argue for two basic components of mindfulness: regulating one's attention to stay in the moment and approaching those moments and our experiences from a place of acceptance. Longtime meditation teacher and author Tara Brach describes this as "recognize and allow" (Brach, n.d.). It might sound simple, but the ability to do this is not at all easy and requires practice and cultivation. This is where mindfulness meditation can help. Studies show that engaging in mindfulness meditation practice on a regular basis can indeed increase the ability to be mindful in the moment (Hölzel et al., 2011).

There are numerous guides for learning to practice mindfulness meditation (classes, books, podcasts, videos, etc.). If you are unfamiliar, the basic aim of mindfulness meditation is to sit quietly for at least a little bit of time each day, focusing your attention on the moment, recognizing thoughts and feelings as they arise, and allowing them to pass along without doing anything or getting caught up in particular trains of thought. Research into mindfulness meditation shows a number of benefits for mental and physical well-being (see Hölzel et al. for a complete listing), but here I will focus on how meditation can improve two key skills: the regulation of attention and the regulation of emotion.

Regulating our attention in the classroom is obviously an important skill. If I am listening closely to my student's comments, for example, I will be able to see how her ideas relate to a larger point I want to get to or to another student's ideas. My close attention to my student is also a signal to her that I care about what she is saying, and this signal is likely to fuel a reciprocal engagement from this student and from others. According to Hölzel et al., the ability to regulate attention better is one of the first skills that novice meditators are able to develop. They refer to this as "conflict monitoring" or "executive attention": the ability to block out distractions while focusing in on a particular object or task. You use this skill, for example, when you keep writing or grading instead of checking the always-so-alluring email. Several studies have now shown that practicing mindfulness meditation (in one case for only five days) improves executive attention and that continued practice may deepen these capabilities. Understanding this science has helped to put words to some of what I have experienced in the classroom since taking up a meditation practice. Put simply, I am better able to focus on what my students are saying and to see the deeper connections between their ideas and the larger ideas we need to uncover rather than being distracted. I am also more likely to see their misperceptions.

In addition to regulating our attention, regulating our emotion is a key skill gained via mindfulness meditation that may be beneficial to our teaching. Research suggests that mindfulness meditation decreases emotional reactivity. That is, we are better able to return to a baseline, calmer state after something upsetting happens or even to avoid feeling overly upset in the first place. One of the ways in which this happens, and something that mindfulness meditation encourages, is reappraisal. Reappraisal refers to "reinterpreting the meaning of a stimulus to change one's emotional response to it" (Hölzel et al., 2011, p. 544). That is, changing how we might normally perceive something so that we perceive it differently. Rather than reflexively becoming angry at a student comment, for example, we are able to change our response, in the moment, into one that is more neutral or even positive. Our closer attention to our emotional reactions allows us to rapidly shift our interpretation toward a more meaningful or useful response.

When I think about this process, I often think about a particular example that relates to the work we do as instructors, though this example actually happened outside the classroom, on a radio call-in show. At the time of the show, same-sex marriage was not yet legal and the discussion I was listening to was about the efforts to legalize it at the state level. This was not long after several states had passed constitutional amendments banning same-sex marriage and many Americans were still opposed to it. On the show, an advocate for same-sex marriage was answering questions from callers and I was in awe of her ability to handle the calls and comments in such a calm and measured way. The real magic of her responses was in how she could take the callers' comments, sometimes filled with misinformation and occasionally with anger, and find something to focus in on to make her larger point. Amazingly, she seemed to both affirm and contradict the callers at the same time, all the while bolstering her main idea: gays and lesbians deserved the right to marry just as much as any other American. It was masterful. And it is something I have thought about many times in facilitating discussion. The skill seems to be one of mindfulness, recognizing and attending closely to what a student (or anyone) is saying and allowing it without reflexive reaction, then following up with a reappraisal before acting or speaking. Given the research linking mindfulness meditation to these key skills, attentional and emotional regulation, it seems to me that investing in some meditation time each day (even as little as 5–10 minutes) could be a useful way to increase our own personal well-being and, perhaps, our effectiveness in teaching about race.

Another way to increase your personal resources is self-affirmation. Try to let go of the Saturday Night Live "Stuart Smalley" idea of self-affirmation (if that reference comes to mind) and instead recall how affirmations were described in Chapters 1 and 2. You may remember that research has consistently shown that when we engage in affirmations of the self we are better at handling threatening or upsetting information. The process seems to happen like this: when we experience threat or when we fail, we feel vulnerable and sometimes out-of-line with how we normally think of ourselves. The threat looms large. Affirmations help us remember that there is more to us than just the threat that we are facing. They help us to broaden our self-view so that the threat or upset becomes a smaller part of a much larger and stronger self (Critcher & Dunning, 2015).

In teaching about race, it can be easy to feel threat. Teaching about race can harm your students' impressions of you and, as we have seen, sometimes your end of semester evaluations as well, a possibility that is especially acute for women of color and for those off the tenure track. Even aside from these larger concerns, the daily experience of teaching about race can be threatening and leave us feeling vulnerable. Tense moments, uncomfortable silences, apathy, conflict, and even just painful cluelessness can make us feel that we are not good teachers. That we are inadequate. Although there is no research (at least not yet) examining how self-affirmations might counteract these feelings for instructors, it seems likely that doing some self-affirmation before we teach could be helpful given the general findings. Most of the research on self-affirmation to this point has focused on writing exercises, specifically, writing for 10–15 minutes about personally important values. Extrapolating a bit from this work as well as from other work on the importance of a sense of purpose or mission, I would offer a couple of suggestions (see the works cited for more information on why these might work):

1. Consider writing for a few minutes at the beginning of the term or prior to an individual class session about your own most important values. Examples of values you might write about include but are not limited to relationships with others, spirituality, science, learning, creativity, and so on. The individual value appears to be less important than letting yourself think about and write about how that value connects you to other people (Shnabel, Purdie-Vaughns, Cook, Garcia, & Cohen, 2013).

2. Think about why you teach what you teach. I know that for many of us, myself included, teaching about race is part of a larger set of goals. We want to help our students see the world more clearly or we want to contribute to the larger cause of social equality. Again, at the beginning of the term or prior to an individual class session, write a few sentences explaining this larger purpose. It might be especially helpful to imagine writing this to another person who is interested in your work and is thinking about doing similar work (Yeager, Henderson, Paunesku, Walton, D'Mello, Spitzer, & Duckworth, 2014).

Protect Your Personal Resources

Our cognitive and emotional energies are finite resources. And even though the science on so-called willpower (or self-regulation) is a bit tangled and unclear with respect to replication issues (Evans, Boggero, & Segerstrom, 2016), the one thing that many agree on and that you have probably seen in yourself is that we do not have an unlimited capacity for self-control. It takes energy to regulate our attention, control our emotions, and make decisions. Without regular rest periods, our capacities diminish, and we may become less able to achieve our goals. As noted throughout this chapter, teaching about race can be emotionally and cognitively difficult. We are juggling our students' emotional responses to what they are learning as well as our own emotional responses. As we are grading, facilitating discussions, and talking to students, we often have to contend with frequent misperceptions and the ways in which students fall back into old ideas or ways of thinking even after we are sure they must have already learned that. All of this takes energy and can be frustrating and depleting.

Knowing more about the psychological research on self-regulation, I have begun to think differently about how I structure my time. I can be news obsessed, particularly when it comes to race, higher education, social policy, and politics. I have learned, though, that I can only handle so much frustration in a given day or week! If I am reading a lot of news and if I am engaging often with Twitter and Facebook, I just have less room for my students. I have not given up reading about the world and trying to follow other people on social media, but I do try to be strategic about it. I do not read comments on news stories. Ever. I avoid both online "debates" and hyper-partisan sources. Finally, I limit my consumption overall and allocate it to specific times during the day. Perhaps these suggestions are obvious, but if you have not considered how you are consuming media and how you feel while you are doing it (does it give you energy versus depleting you), then you may not be using your energy in a strategic way. Given that your students are more likely to learn than those you interact with on social media, don't they deserve your best attention and efforts?

In addition to media consumption, it might also be useful to observe yourself for a few days to determine when your energy is higher and when you feel best. You can do this easily using a paper record or via the notes app on your phone. Given the malleability of human memory, it makes sense to try to do this in the moment and as you go through your day for several weekdays. Just answer these questions: What am I doing? How am I feeling? You can use a simple 1 (very low energy) to 10 (very high energy) scale or more descriptive phrases, but whatever you do just try to get your feelings and activities recorded. Like many people (though certainly not all), I am more energetic in the mornings. As a result, I have tried to shift my writing and teaching to the mornings rather than the afternoons, leaving those times for email and committee work. Though these measures may not be available to everyone, I believe they are worth pursing where possible. It is important that we take control over how we use our energy and how we structure our work environments. Our own well-being and the learning of our students is worth it, and I believe we should be unapologetic about asking for what we need so that our students can benefit.

Work to Increase Your Community and Administrative Resources

Earlier, when describing the importance of knowing the content, I cited a study published by Pasque, Chesler, Charbeneau, and Carlson (2013). For that work, the authors interviewed a diverse and wide range of instructors who reported on how they handle racial conflict in the classroom. Only some of these instructors explicitly taught about race, but all had faced racial tension or conflict in the course of their teaching. The authors gave several suggestions for how to help faculty work through these conflicts, but ultimately, they also pointed out that individual actions are not enough. We can do a lot for ourselves, but we should not always have to do it alone. Instead, they called for academic leaders to support more faculty development opportunities around race or racial conflict and for faculty to work together to create "a small teaching counterculture" (p. 13).

Echoing these ideas, Ahluwalia et al. (in press) found that all 12 of the instructors of Multicultural Competence that they interviewed cited departmental or program support as critically important. Even when that support was mandated through an accreditation process, it mattered. Some of the specific things cited by interviewees as helpful included mission statements that explicitly endorse increasing diversity, the intentional recruitment of students of color, and administrators who are visibly supportive. For example, one participant wrote about how the department had intentionally conducted additional classroom observations of her teaching to help balance out any possible negative student evaluations. She was also encouraged to include more explanation about the course in her tenure file as a way to help colleagues understand why lower evaluations might happen. Such efforts by department chairs, deans, or program directors directly communicate an understanding of the difficulty of teaching about race and an expectation that others understand and respect that difficulty.

In addition to administrative support, we can also work to create our own teaching countercultures and networks. Over the years, I have found it deeply helpful to connect with others who teach about race. I have not always done a great job of keeping up with everyone, but I have tried to maintain at least some relationship to others who do this work via Facebook groups and email and with the occasional get-together on campus or at academic conferences. Sharing resources, discussing teaching, and copresenting have all been instrumental in helping me feel less alone and more committed to teaching well. Note, also, that even if you are on a small campus, you can still find allies in those who teach other resistance-prone topics. I have formed friendships with those who teach about evolution, politics, immigration, climate change, and a host of other issues. Bonding over shared student resistance can be a great way to find common ground with faculty from disciplines you might otherwise assume are very different from your own. For example, on my own campus I have been able to connect with faculty from our agricultural college. Some of them teach about race as well (immigration and agriculture), but others teach about different resistance-prone topics (environmental science). Through this collaboration we have created workshops on teaching development for other instructors and all of these colleagues have become important allies on campus in raising awareness about racism more generally amongst our faculty and staff.

On a structural level, it is important that those who facilitate faculty professional development take up these concerns and provide opportunities for faculty to gain skills and learn from the research and wisdom of other instructors. Sometimes you can help create these experiences yourself, hosting a roundtable or panel discussion on teaching about race at an academic conference, setting up book or article discussion groups on your own campus, and conducting and presenting your own scholarship of teaching work, but it is also important to advocate for more support from academic leaders and centers for teaching and learning (if your campus supports one). Given the current political climate and the recent increase in campus activism and protest, this is an important time to advocate for instructor support, and academic leaders should be asked to provide that support.

You may recall that in the case of Shannon Gibney, reprimanded for her teaching about institutional racism, her college stated the following: "We expect that faculty will have the professional skills to lead difficult conversations in their classrooms and will teach in a way that helps students understand issues, even when students feel uncomfortable or disagree with particular ideas" (Flaherty, 2013, p. 3). My guess is that many institutions hope faculty will have or will develop these skills, but most are probably not providing concrete assistance. Academic leaders, including presidents, provosts, and deans can and should be pressed to support this kind of professional development. If you advocate for such programs, be sure to note any campus climate data you may have access to (which often shows how uncomfortable both faculty and students are around race in the classroom) or examples from the news that may be relevant. Be sure, as well, to note the disproportionate toll that such teaching takes on instructors of color (Ahluwalia et al., in press). Those who are marginalized by race need more support than their White counterparts because they face more pushback and more difficulty. One final note: I would strongly recommend structuring any faculty development you pursue to include both workshops as well as cohorts. Faculty fellows' programs, communities of practice, or teaching circles that allow for the same small group to work together over time to think through their teaching around race are likely to provide more support and create the kinds of transformative experiences that lead to real growth and change in the classroom.

—

Chapter 4

BELONGING IN THE CLASSROOM: CREATING MOMENTS OF POSITIVITY AND CONNECTION

—

IN THE SPRING OF 2006, I found myself on a panel with other instructors of psychology at a small, regional teaching conference. I had not put together the panel myself and did not know any of the other instructors. All of us were chosen because we taught about race at our respective institutions and the idea was for us to talk about how best to do that. Just before we started, I had a conversation with one of the other panelists who told me that her overall approach to teaching about race could be summed up in one phrase that she often repeated to her students: "I don't have an opinion; I have a PhD." I understood immediately what she meant, but I also felt uneasy.

On the one hand, the need to establish our expertise is important. As noted in Chapter 1, those of us who teach about race have typically devoted years of our lives to understanding it from within our particular disciplines. We also know that many Americans are unaware of (or unwilling to believe) some of the basics when it comes to race. American individualism as well as our colorblind norms and ideals do not leave a lot of room for understanding how institutional and structural factors shape our lives when it comes to our own race, the race of others, and the larger system of White supremacy within which we all find ourselves. As I have noted repeatedly, understanding that this larger system exists is often *the* critical step that students need to make in order to get beyond individualistic conceptions of race (e.g., racism as individual prejudice or isolated acts of open hostility) and toward a more complete understanding of how powerful racism and White supremacy are in determining life outcomes. The denial of these realities is a much more comfortable place for many Americans, especially those who are White, and so pre-emptively trying to tamp down this denial with a strong statement of expertise may feel logical and necessary.

On the other hand, however, instructors hold a lot of power in the classroom. We set the agenda and award the grades. When we double down on this power by explicitly stating, "I know it, you do not," we risk creating feelings of alienation and anger. We risk the perception that we are using our power in a coercive and illegitimate way (Cavanagh, 2016). From the students' perspective, this kind of statement makes it clear that our thoughts and feelings will take precedence over theirs and that perhaps they cannot be right unless they agree with us and with our course content. This may feel okay; after all, we know the material much better right? The problem is that none of us likes to have our feelings or thoughts dismissed. It impinges on our autonomy, which is key to motivation, and can increase our defensiveness, reducing the possibility of connection. Why should I share my experiences or thoughts when I know that I could be told that I am wrong?

Walking this line between being forthright about the realities of racism while also making space for our students to have their own feelings is, to me, the key pedagogical challenge in teaching about race. No solution is perfect and not every student will learn or be willing to learn, even in the best of situations. The very nature of our subject will mean that some students, especially White students, will project a confrontational stance onto us despite our best efforts to use our power carefully and well. How to walk this line? I believe that confrontation, shame, and anger demotivate learning. They do not work in the classroom. At the same time, positivity and connection increase motivation and empower students to learn. So, while it may feel very tempting to simply push through the content without a lot of input, especially when you know their input is likely to be wrong, it does not serve our larger purpose. It really is in our best overall interest to create a classroom atmosphere that is positive and open, encouraging feelings of connection and belonging.

To show how this might work, I begin this chapter by reviewing recent evidence from social psychology with respect to positivity and belonging. As I continue, I will connect these ideas to learning and review a few of the studies that have connected feelings of belonging to academic success. I will also tackle the questions of shame, blame, and guilt. Research with respect to interventions for both racism and sexism have suggested that approaches relying on these emotions are often counterproductive. Throughout, I will try to show how these ideas could translate into the classroom and will end the chapter with specific suggestions. My hope is that each of us can successfully walk a middle path in our classrooms: retaining our authority, being uncompromising and ruthlessly honest with respect to the content, but also attentive and sensitive to the atmosphere we create.

One last point before we dig in. I want to acknowledge how good it can feel to hold our expertise and to bond with our colleagues over how much we know as compared to most of our students. If we are being honest, there are times when we revel in the cluelessness of our students as we talk to each other. This is understandable. Sometimes student comments are truly ludicrous, upsetting, and even jaw dropping in their lack of understanding (recall the example I described earlier in which a student equated Black Lives Matter with the KKK). The stress of working with such comments is part of why we need to take steps to care for ourselves and to protect our limited energy and attention. It is also why it can be helpful to connect with colleagues and create networks of like-minded instructors. We need to see that we are not alone. The danger, however, is in the possible dehumanization of our students. When we engage in snarky conversations about the ignorance of our students, post student comments on social media for others to laugh at or comment on, or trade student-shaming stories over lunch or coffee, we may feel better at the risk of our own ability to understand where our students are coming from. In those moments, it may feel very good and very validating to bond with our colleagues, but engaging in this kind of talk regularly can make it hard to hold space for students and to allow them to ask questions or make comments without quick and harsh judgment. If, when my student conflates the Black Lives Matter movement with the KKK, I am more focused on sharing that story with colleagues or thinking about how upsetting and ridiculous this idea is, I am less able in that moment to slow down and try to see where he is coming from. I do not have the space to respond in a thoughtful way.

Drawing this example out further, if I am continually discussing student cluelessness about race with my colleagues, family, and friends, then a comment like this *is* going to seem ridiculous. Responding in that mindset, shaming him or simply ignoring it and chalking it up to stupidity, provides no possibility for further learning. The more difficult, and perhaps more rewarding path is to pause (again, we have to have the personal resources to do this) and remember that this attitude about the Black Lives Matter movement is probably not all that unusual given the student's White identity (Pew Research, 2016), that it makes some sense in the context of what this student knows or has been exposed to. Instead of shaming or ignoring, I can take the opportunity to try and correct his misunderstanding in a calm and nonjudgmental way. In doing that, I model my own expertise, citing sources, and I also communicate acceptance and positivity toward the student. This still may not result in learning (some students are stubborn in their resistance or want to remain willfully inaccurate in the face of evidence), but I am at least providing the opportunity to learn, and I am letting that student know that I care about their learning. Helpful too: I am not fulfilling the stereotype of the "liberal, indoctrinating academic" that pervades our larger media. In short, I am accepting my student while still providing accurate information that tells the truth about the extent of American racism.

POSITIVITY

In her 2013 book *Love 2.0*, psychologist Barbara Fredrickson describes a new way to think about love, positive emotion, and our connection to others. She argues that positive emotions (joy, gratitude, hope, amusement, etc.) are essential to a broader and more expansive outlook. Even when brief or experienced only in moments, these feelings help us to see things differently and open us up to new ideas and new knowledge. We become more flexible. Her model for this overall process is the "broaden-and-build theory of positive emotion" (p. 8), and the evidence in support of this theory has accumulated across a variety of outcomes since its initial publication in 1998 (Fredrickson, 2013). For example, increased feelings of positivity quite literally widen visual attention. Study participants shown positive images (a puppy for example) were more likely to report seeing not just that object but also the context surrounding that object whereas those in more negative emotional states saw less. Measurements of neural blood flow patterns confirmed these differences, showing how our brains differ depending on our emotional state to either widen or narrow our perception (Fredrickson, 2013). Other work has shown how positive emotions can increase our openness to new experiences and to critical feedback (Fredrickson, Cohn, Coffey, Pek, & Finkel, 2008). As we broaden our focus in the wake of positive feeling, we are able to build up our personal resources, developing and improving on our social, cognitive, and psychological abilities. Applied to the classroom, it seems likely that investing in positivity could result in increased attention and resilience in the face of difficult content.

In support of this idea, Sarah Cavanagh argues throughout her 2016 book *The Spark of Learning* that emotions play a critical role in learning. She cites numerous studies and describes in detail how different emotions can influence our attention, our motivation to learn, and our memory. She focuses on a variety of emotional states, both positive and negative, but it is clear that most of the evidence to date suggests an important role for positivity. Enthusiasm, confidence, optimism, and the like can create a "crossover" effect whereby a teacher's behavior changes in positive ways (teaching with more clarity, giving more examples) which then shifts how students feel about the class, increasing their motivation and performance. In describing how positive emotion can influence the classroom, Cavanaugh outlines a variety of routes we might take to increase positivity in the classroom. These include enthusiasm, humor, warmth, and optimism, but here I want to zoom in on the particular importance of belonging and connection.

Belonging and Connection

If you take a moment to reflect, can you recall a time when you felt happiest in your relationship with a loved one? A particular instant? The chances are good that you were looking at them, perhaps touching and leaning in close. I myself have vivid memories of looking at my young son as he smiled back at me in moments of joy or wonder. That sharing of feeling seems to be a key ingredient in creating the bonds of love we share with other people. As Fredrickson argues throughout her aforementioned book, *Love 2.0*, love is really about micro-moments of connection, experienced repeatedly, that ripple out to influence our subsequent feelings and behavior. It may seem odd to reference the notion of love in a book about teaching, but as I have learned more about student retention and success in recent years, it has become clear to me that connecting with our students and helping them connect to each other is an important way to increase student enjoyment and positive feeling. Moreover, according to Fredrickson, such feelings do not have to be intense. It is true that it is often easier to remember such important moments (here again, remembering my son's sweet little face), but it is not necessary for every moment to rise to that level. Instead, we can cultivate micro-moments every day in our classes. Moments that communicate connection, thereby cultivating positivity. The phrase used in the literature to describe this process is belonging or a sense of belonging.

Before describing some of the research, it is important to note why belonging seems to matter so much in the first place. Put simply, belonging provides us with a sense that we matter and that we are part of something larger than we are. As a result, the desire to belong appears to be a fundamental human drive and research has shown that those with a stronger sense of belonging are also more likely to report a stronger sense of meaning in their lives (Lambert, Stillman, Hicks, Kamble, Baumeister, & Fincham, 2013). Conversely, not belonging or being excluded from others can lead to a host of negative physical and mental health outcomes.

One of the first studies to examine how an increased sense of belonging might improve the experience of college students was published in *Science* in 2011. That influential study, conducted by Stanford professors Gregory M. Walton and Geoffrey L. Cohen, followed 92 first-year students as part of a randomized control trial lasting 3 years. Both Black and White students participated, with half reading about the experiences of upper-level students and the struggles they faced as first-year students (treatment), while the other half read about attitude change (control). The treatment group read several quotes and stories, all reinforcing a very clear theme: everyone struggles their first year in college, but most people overcome these struggles. The idea was to help students see that they are not alone in their feelings and that everyone, regardless of race, has a similar experience of struggle. To reinforce the lesson, these treatment students then wrote about their own experiences and made a short video about these experiences for future students. The results were striking. Though the White students were unaffected by condition (they performed well after both the control and treatment conditions), the Black students in the treatment condition showed significant GPA increases over time (as compared to the control condition Black students) and the usual achievement gap between Black and White students was cut in half. After 3 years, all of the students completed a survey. The results showed that Black students in the treatment condition were happier, healthier, had fewer doctor visits, and felt less uncertainty about their belonging as compared to Black students in the control condition. Again, White students had positive outcomes after both conditions. They were unaffected.

These findings were remarkable. In total, the intervention lasted about an hour and most participants were unable to recall the details of the intervention 3 years later. But that hour resulted in significant differences in college achievement and well-being. Since that study, there have been many others, including one published in 2016 that examined how a similar intervention affected the retention and success of over 7,000 students (Yeager et al., 2016). The particulars of this study are different given its much larger scale, but the gist was the same. In the belonging intervention condition, students received the message (this time delivered via computer) that older students had once struggled but had overcome those struggles. The participants did not make a video, but they did write about how their own experiences matched those they had read about, and they were told that their responses might be shared with others. The results showed that those most at risk of dropping out (low-income students, minority students) were more likely to continue full-time enrollment and were more likely to report making close friends in college, using academic services, and joining extracurricular activities as compared to those in the control condition. Just as in the earlier study, increased academic and social integration resulted from a simple intervention.

To understand why a short, otherwise unremarkable intervention might pack such a powerful punch, it is important to understand how bolstering one's sense of belonging can change our perception. When the students in Walton and Cohen's original 2011 study went back to their residence halls after the initial intervention, they contributed diary entries for about a week in answer to the same set of questions each day. They reported their daily experiences of adversity and their daily sense of belonging. For White students and for Black students who received the intervention, there was no relationship between these two factors. That is, their experiences of adversity were unrelated to their feelings of belonging on campus. For Black students in the control condition, however, there was a consistent finding of lower belonging on days of increased adversity. For these students, adversity was a signal that they might not belong. This makes sense when you consider the pervasive stereotype that surrounds Black students—namely, that they are not as academically talented or prepared. The trick of the belonging intervention, according to the authors, is how it "untether[ed] their sense of belonging from daily hardship" (Walton & Cohen, 2011, p. 1449). After reading about others' experiences and seeing how those experiences might match their own, these students were able to interpret hardship as a more normal process and not as something that indicated their own lack of ability or fulfillment of stereotypes. Subsequent, similar research with other social groups (Brady et al., 2016; Stephens, Townsend, Hamedani, Destin, & Manzo, 2015) has replicated this pattern, illustrating how an intervention can alter the interpretation of adversity to improve student outcomes years after an initial intervention. If you want to learn more about the power of such interventions, I would urge you to check out the Mindset Scholars Network (http://mindsetscholarsnetwork.org).

Belonging in the Classroom

Unsurprisingly, given the research described above, feelings of belonging in class can increase student integration and engagement. In describing the research, I will focus on a few main areas of work: our students' connection to us as instructors, sometimes called instructor rapport; their connections to each other; and the ways in which the environment can signal belonging.

Writing in 2015 in *Teaching of Psychology*, Daniel T. Rogers defined instructor rapport in a way that reminds me a lot of how Barbara Fredrickson (2013) talks about love and connection. Rogers states that instructor-student rapport comprises "positive, synchronous interactions that reflect closeness or connectedness" (p. 20). In other words, connecting in small ways over time that may accumulate. Micromoments, as Fredrickson termed them. In studying feelings of instructor-student rapport, Wilson and Ryan (2013) found that strong feelings of rapport positively predicted students' motivation, likelihood of coming to class, perceptions that they had learned, and final grades. If we look closely at how these authors measured student feelings of rapport, it gives us an excellent starting point for working to create rapport in our classes. It turns out that the most predictive items on their Professor-Student Rapport Scale were focused on how professors make students feel: "my professor encourages questions and comments from students," "my professor's body language says, 'don't bother me'" (reverse scored), and "my professor makes the class enjoyable." Previous research on rapport has focused on the nonverbal behavior of teachers as well as the likeability or enthusiasm of the professor. This study measured those elements, too, but in the end, what mattered most for actual student outcomes was not really how much students liked the professor, but rather what professors did to make a class feel open, a space where questions are encouraged, and students are not worried that they might be bugging us. None of this work, at least from what I could see, directly assessed how rapport connected to feelings of student belonging. However, the definition of rapport and the findings of Wilson and Ryan certainly suggest that such feelings are likely to be present as rapport increases and that rapport itself helps to increase student learning. The next set of studies assesses classroom belonging more directly, shows how it relates to those micromoments of connection, and provides us with another tool for improving learning.

When you walk into a classroom, are the students chatting with each other? Do you chat with people before a meeting starts? At a very basic level, despite whatever we may or may not have in common with the people around us, interacting with them is generally a good thing to do. Research suggests that these little interactions increase our well-being and happiness (Sandstrom & Dunn, 2014a). There are, of course, probably exceptions to this (social anxiety, bad days) but in the last few years, social psychologist Gillian Sandstrom has been investigating how these little moments of interaction, even with "weak ties" or people we do not know well, improve our well-being because they increase our sense of belonging. When I first started reading this work, it was striking to me how nicely the conclusions matched Frederickson (2013) and her notions of positivity and connection. Both sets of research focus on the importance of micro-moments and how these small moments can accumulate and ripple out to improve our lives. In the case of our classrooms, Sandstrom's work is particularly helpful.

In a study published in 2014 (Sandstrom & Dunn, 2014b), students were recruited from a set of large, introductory courses at the University of British Columbia. The students responded to text message prompts at six points throughout the semester. These messages asked them to list how many interactions they had had with others, how happy they felt, and how much they felt that they belonged. A final survey asked them how many people they knew and asked them to classify those folks as "strong" ties or "weak" ties. The results showed that the more the students interacted with others in class, the happier they felt. This happened regardless of personality (so it was not about being extraverted) and happened even when the only interactions they experienced were with weak ties. In other words, interacting with others in class was enough to increase happiness and a sense of belonging even when those others were not close friends.

In another published study, Sandstrom and Rawn (2015) were able to show just how important these feelings of belonging can be. This time, the researchers again recruited students from across several large, introductory courses and asked them to fill out a few quick measures after class via text message. At six points throughout the semester, the students listed how many people they had interacted with during class, how much they enjoyed the class, and how much they felt that they belonged. They also answered an extensive end-of-semester survey that assessed their overall course enjoyment and sense of belonging. Finally, the researcher got permission to access their final grades. In keeping with the earlier study, the results showed that on days when students reported more interaction, they also reported a stronger sense of belonging and greater enjoyment of class. Importantly, though, those daily interactions and subsequent increases in sense of belonging also predicted overall course enjoyment. In other words, if I interact with my fellow students, even in off-topic ways, I feel more belonging, which then leads to greater course enjoyment. The order is important. Belonging seems to come first and to develop because of those daily interactions. The results for grades followed the same trend, though they were not statistically significant. That is, as students interacted more on a daily basis, their feelings of belonging rose in tandem. Those feelings of belonging were then marginal predictors of final grades.

A later study, conducted by myself and my co-authors Wei Zheng and Tricia Davis (2014), was able to show a stronger tie between feelings of overall classroom belonging and student learning. In our work, conducted across three classes focused on race and diversity, we were able to show that overall course belonging correlated with three different types of learning: increased awareness of racial privilege and discrimination, students' perceptions of their own learning, and the average grade for key assignments in each course. Taken together, these studies point towards an important recommendation for instructors: we should work to increase student-to-student interactions because those moments of connection can ripple out, increasing belonging and positivity and possibly improving student learning.

In addition to the people around us, the environment itself can signal a lot about belonging. Think about how you feel as you enter various spaces: an unfamiliar office, a place of worship, a store. It is likely the objects you encounter in those spaces will either communicate a sense of familiarity or a sense that you are in new territory. Sapna Cheryan and her colleagues call this "ambient belonging" (Cheryan, Plaut, Davies, & Steele, 2009). Across several experiments, these researchers were able to show how simple objects scattered around a testing room could increase female students' sense of belonging and subsequent interest in particular majors or job opportunities. For example, environments that were not stereotypical with respect to computer science (nature posters, coffee mugs, water bottles) consistently improved female students' interest in computer science as compared to more stereotypical environments (soda cans, Star Trek posters). Importantly, the women's sense of belonging was what mattered for these effects. When describing the findings of a different, but similar experiment in the same paper, the authors write that "women were driven away from a job opportunity (even one in which men were entirely absent) because the stereotypical nature of the environment communicated to them that they would not belong" (p. 1051). So, what do our environments communicate? Is there a way to use simple cues to suggest that we are similar to our students or that they belong? I do not have specific answers to these questions, but the findings of Cheryan and her colleagues make me want to think a little harder about what I am communicating to my students, even via simple objects. Since reading these studies and thinking more about their implications, I have worked harder to find points of connection with my students. Given the potential power of belonging for student learning and success, this effort seems well worth it.

So where are we at this point? We know that feelings of positivity can widen our view and open us to new information, even information that is uncomfortable or self-critical.

We have also seen how important positivity is for connection and belonging. When students feel that they belong, their learning may improve, and they become more persistent and successful overall. At the same time, we know how negative and difficult learning about racism can be. Students are often resistant to learning about race because it can make them feel powerless and angry (often the case for students of color) or guilty and angry (often the case for White students). Before we leave this chapter, it is important to take a closer and more detailed look at the negative experiences of blame and guilt. Research has shown us that these emotions can be counterproductive when it comes to learning about racism and that at least part of the reason for this is because such feelings sever connection and belonging.

BLAME, GUILT, AND NEGATIVITY

In many ways, guilt, particularly on the part of White students, is to be expected and is a normal response to learning about racism. Beverly Daniel Tatum, in her 2017 book on race and identity *Why Are All the Black Kids Sitting Together in the Cafeteria?*, describes in detail how the racial identification process proceeds for White students. She does this by showing how her students' own experiences fit with and illustrated the stages of racial identification initially spelled out by the scholar Janet Helms. According to Helms, guilt is a predictable and inevitable part of the identification process for White students, particularly after the initial stages of disbelief recede. In my own work, I have also shown how White guilt increases as a result of learning about racism (Chick, Karis, & Kernahan, 2009; Kernahan & Davis, 2007), and I have witnessed, as an instructor, how guilt can ebb and flow for White students over the course of the semester.

I believe it is important, though, to distinguish between guilt as a *part* of the process of learning and guilt as the *point* of the process of learning. There is no question that for some, guilt or even shame are a desirable outcome. Timothy Wilson, in his 2011 book *Redirect*, describes the techniques of Jane Elliott ("blue eyes-brown eyes" activity) and the ways in which her interventions to reduce prejudice could induce strong feelings of self-focused anger and discomfort (if you have seen the films of her work with adults, you understand this well). As Wilson notes, there is only one randomized controlled study of this technique. The results showed that several of those assigned to the activity dropped out because of their discomfort. Of those who remained, there was a significant increase in self-focused anger with respect to holding prejudiced attitudes, but no significant reduction in racist attitudes.

Recent work helps us understand why her techniques did not work to reduce racist attitudes. In 2014, Corrine A. Moss-Racusin and her colleagues published a review of the evidence on effective bias interventions. In taking a more scientific approach, these scientists were hoping to provide evidence-based ideas in an area (diversity training) that is often lacking in rigorous assessment. One of the main findings of their review was that interventions to reduce bias can often induce backlash, increasing rather than decreasing prejudice. This backlash, they argued, is most likely when participants feel 1) pressured into adopting anti-biased attitudes and/or 2) blamed for their own bias and prejudice. Given what we have covered in this chapter, this is not terribly surprising. Not only are coercion and blame negative feelings, which may constrict rather than widen our perspective, but these feelings are also very self-focused, moving us away from connection to others and, perhaps, preventing us from seeing the larger picture of institutional racism.

To expand these ideas further, it might be helpful to see how some instructors have applied these insights and worked effectively with their students to get beyond blame. Patrick and Connolly published a paper in 2013 describing how they helped their graduate-level counseling students learn more about racial privilege. As part of the course, they used a series of nine assigned questions to guide their discussions. Later, they analyzed the students' anonymous responses to those questions across several semesters. There were many interesting aspects to their approach and findings, but I want to highlight one point in particular: the importance of externalization with respect to the process of learning about privilege. The instructors asked their students to think not so much about how they themselves are privileged but rather how privilege might influence their lives and the lives of others. It may seem like a small distinction, but given how ineffective self-blame can be, it is important. Asking students to think about the problems of privilege as problems that fluctuate and can shift according to external conditions rather than as some sort of stable, internal trait (e.g., "I am privileged") seemed to help students understand the issue and, most importantly, understand it in institutional forms rather than individual meanness. To be clear, these instructors did not shy away from shame or guilt. One of their nine assigned questions asked students to reflect on these feelings directly, and most of the students reported experiencing both shame and guilt. The difference, however, was that students seemed able to move beyond these feelings and onto larger insights around more systemic forms of racism and privilege. In other words, the students did not get stuck thinking about themselves and their own privilege, they were pushed to think more systemically, and their learning increased as a result.

Feeling Bad Can Diminish Connection and Belonging

Another fascinating exploration of negativity in teaching about race comes from the Midwest Critical Whiteness Collective. Writing in the *Harvard Educational Review* in 2013, Lensmire, McManimon, Tierney, Lee-Nichols, Casey, Lensmire, and Davis argue against what they see as an often-exclusive focus on learning about White privilege at the expense of learning about White racism. There are a variety of interesting points and critiques contained in this paper, but I found myself especially struck by two ideas. First, they note that there is often a focus in teaching about race to White students on the "confession" of White privilege. That is, instructors focus on the confessions of their White students as a key outcome, as if somehow getting them to admit that they are privileged is the most important outcome of the course. The problem with this, however, is that individual confession and contrition can take attention away from the larger forces at work. Students, especially White students, can simply view themselves as better people if they have "confessed." Having admitted that they are personally privileged or that they feel guilty, they are free to exempt themselves from the larger system of institutional racism. As a result, there is less focus on understanding the importance of institutional racism and students are not really learning beyond themselves. As Lensmire et al. (2013) state, "white privilege is not the cause of racial differentiation and structures: it is the effect of the socially, politically, and economically constructed system that we call race" (p. 421).

A second key point made in this article involves the ways in which students' reactions to the notion of privilege can set them apart from us as instructors and from their classmates. In the course of the paper, the authors profile an instructor of multicultural education named Mary who is struggling with a student named John. In learning about racial privilege, John expresses a lot of resistance. Like many of us, Mary initially hopes to get John to admit to his privilege and to see the ways in which he (a White, male student) benefits from racism. She wants him to understand White privilege in the way that she does and to understand how he has benefitted. Ultimately, though, Mary realizes that John is not an outlier. She has taught other students who do not feel that the reading on privilege (Peggy McIntosh's 1988 "knapsack" article) resonates for them. As a poor person, John has experienced a lot of class-based disadvantage and so many of the privileges listed do not necessarily apply to him or to other students. The focus on privilege from such an individual perspective, just the author's experiences, can make it difficult for some students to relate, especially early on in a course. For some students the idea that they are privileged just feels "wrong." As Mary re-examines the reading on privilege from his perspective, she decides to let go of privilege confession as a teaching outcome. Instead, she focuses on getting to know John better and on his understanding of racism more broadly.

By the end of the semester, Mary finds that despite his inability to confess his privilege, John has learned a lot about racial disadvantage. Furthermore, his racial attitudes have shifted. He has become an advocate for refugees and he opposes the use of Native American mascots for sports teams. He also describes a newfound skepticism about how those in the media vilify immigrants. There is not a direct comparison available here, but I do not think it is a stretch to say that Mary could have easily fallen into a continuing conflict with this student. In that scenario, if she had not worked to maintain an understanding of her student, it seems unlikely that he would have learned as much as he did. In that scenario, the tug-of-war over personal confession would have taken up space better used for learning. Furthermore, an early breach of connection between student and instructor could have set off a spiral of mistrust that would make learning difficult even after moving on from privilege. If he felt judged for his disagreements with the content so early on, why would he trust later content?

You may be thinking, "but wait, he *is* privileged as a White, male student," and that is true, of course. The question, though, is one of importance: would seeing (and admitting) that he is privileged really help John to understand overall systems of racial bias? I am not sure that it would, particularly so early in the semester. Furthermore, we run the risk of alienating such students before they have had a chance to learn. Because connection matters, I think we would be smart to really think about our learning goals and choose our battles accordingly. In this case, understanding John as a person and drawing him out about his own experiences of socioeconomic disadvantage were ultimately affirming and probably helped improve his feelings of trust and belonging, ultimately helping him learn as much as he did. It seems clear in this case that allowing a marginalized social identity and emphasizing the intersectional nature of privilege and disadvantage may lead to less threat and more learning.

One last point on this example that I believe is important: when students do not share in the emotional reactions of their classmates (and John did not), they run the risk of being cut off not only from us as instructors but also from their student colleagues. A student in that situation, feeling as though she sees things very differently from everyone else, is likely to be defensive and even more resistant to learning. By seeking to maintain a connection with such students, especially early on in the course, we increase the chances that these students can feel included and affirmed, ultimately increasing the likelihood they will learn. What this means in practice is maintaining connection with our students and being gentle in how we point out differences in understanding in front of the whole class.

Does Shame Have a Place?

In the days after the 2016 election of Donald Trump, hate crimes increased rapidly (more than 1,000 in the first month according to the Southern Poverty Law Center, 2016), and it seemed that many people felt a new "freedom" to express angry and biased feelings. The pointed and openly biased rhetoric coming from the Republican nominee and eventual president stood in sharp contrast to that of recent presidents and candidates. Social psychologists studying attitudes before and after the election showed that participants felt an increase in the acceptability of biases towards Muslims, immigrants, Mexicans, fat people, and people with disabilities. Participants also felt that these biases were more acceptable than biases against other groups who were not discussed much during the campaign (e.g., alcoholics) (Crandall & White, 2016).

As the norms shifted, I noticed an interesting conversation popping up in my Twitter feed and in the popular media. The question posed often went something like this: Isn't shame a good thing? When people feel free to express racism, doesn't that normalize it, making it more likely that people will feel free to act on their biases? If so, isn't it important to push back on our changing norms, calling out and sometimes shaming those who perpetuate racist ideas? As a social psychologist, I certainly understand that norms and sanctions matter. There is much evidence and theory to show that people emulate the norms for behavior that they see around them (e.g., social learning theory). But social psychologists also understand that context matters. Shaming someone on Twitter or Facebook or even during a one-on-one discussion is not the same thing as a student being shamed by a teacher within a classroom. Within a classroom, a teacher has power and I believe that using that power to shame is counterproductive if our goal is to help students learn.

As noted earlier, most of the research that has been done on interventions to reduce prejudice tells us the same story: forcing or pressuring people to change their attitudes through external pressure and the threat of shame or sanction typically just results in backlash. Instead of increasing understanding or changing attitudes for the better, we see increases in prejudice instead (Legault, Gutsell, & Inzlicht, 2011; Moss-Racusin et al., 2014). The power we have as teachers is not effective if we are using it to make students feel bad. Rather than being open to learning, most people in this situation constrict their focus inward into unproductive guilt or rebellion (or both).

As teachers, we want to be clear about what is true and what is not with respect to the realities of racism. It can be very frustrating to know that we have presented information well and fairly and still be met with disbelief and resistance. We may want to push back hard or allow other students to make snide comments to those who are less far along in their understanding. But this is counterproductive. We will get further if we provide a relatively positive environment and encourage students to connect to us and to each other. There are cases where these techniques may not work, students who will continue to resist despite our best efforts, but the evidence suggests that, in general, focusing on creating moments of connection and positivity rather than blame and shame will enhance learning and minimize backlash effects.

SUMMARIZED RECOMMENDATIONS AND SUGGESTIONS

Create and Maintain a Positive Classroom Climate

Remember that there are lots of possibilities for creating and maintaining positivity. I believe that belonging and connection are particularly important in our work, but there are additional routes to positivity and many are outlined and explained nicely in Sarah Cavanagh's 2016 book *The Spark of Learning*. As Cavanagh notes, humor, optimism, and enthusiasm can all improve student learning. I myself am not a particularly optimistic or sunny person, but I am enthusiastic about my courses and I try to convey that in how I talk about the content. I am honest about how much I love it, about how long I have spent studying it, and that I genuinely enjoy (mostly) the process of talking about and teaching about race and racism with students.

Since I am not a natural comedian, I also use the humor of others to help increase positivity in the classroom. When it comes to race, there is no shortage of good content that satirizes race and the ways in which we deal (or don't deal) with race in the United States. To capitalize on this, I have shown clips of skits that skewer stereotypes about race (*The Dave Chappelle Show, Saturday Night Live, MTV Decoded*) or illustrate important problems of racism through humor (John Oliver's *Last Week Tonight*). Even more fun is when I have asked students to post and share their own examples online or in class. One year I did this as part of the final for the course, asking students to post a clip and then requesting that they briefly introduce the clip in class by describing what they enjoyed about it and how they saw it as connected to what they had learned. This kind of assignment not only allows for humor, but also student autonomy and control, a double attempt at creating positivity. Again, I would recommend checking out Sarah Cavanagh's book on learning and emotion to glean other tips.

Create Moments of Connection

As noted by psychologist Barbara Fredrickson, we experience important and consequential ripples of positive emotion when we experience moments of connection to others. Some basic elements of this involve making eye contact, asking questions, moving our bodies to be on the same level as others, and finding ways to share points of similarity. As noted earlier, many of these behaviors have been referred to as teacher-student rapport (Rogers, 2015). And just to be clear (especially for those steeped in the teaching and learning literature), rapport is not the same thing as "immediacy," a related but distinct concept that focuses more on the psychological availability or nearness of an instructor. Research has shown that immediacy is important, but probably not as predictive of course enjoyment or learning as rapport and connection (Rogers, 2015; Wilson & Ryan, 2013). To create the positive classroom environment we seek, we may want to start early in building rapport and connection.

The first day can be especially critical to how students perceive and feel about our courses and about us as instructors (McGinley & Jones, 2014). Despite my own introversion and fear, I always conduct first- and second-day getting-to-know you exercises that involve having the students speak to each other in small groups to answer a variety of questions, some related to course material and others just for fun. As they talk, I walk around the room, checking in with each group and explicitly practicing their names to try and get them right. I try to take my time with this, making eye contact and using whatever cues I can to draw out the similarities between my students and myself. Maybe they have a jacket on that signifies their gym membership (hey, I go to the gym too) or they are discussing a television show (one of my icebreaker questions) that I love or hate or do not know anything about. Whatever the case, I try to find a way to connect, just briefly, make eye contact, smile, and let them know that I care about knowing their name (even as I fail at getting it right the first few times). With an eye toward the student-rapport findings cited earlier, I try to maintain these kinds of connections throughout the course, aiming to send the message "I see you, you matter."

Create a Space for Students to Connect to Each Other

Perhaps your experience is different, but I have found that most often when I enter a classroom it is quiet. Students are snapping or texting (or doing whatever is cool by the time you read this) and typically not talking with one another. Given what we now know about student-to-student interaction and its connection to belonging, enjoyment, motivation, and learning, it is imperative to try and get them talking. In addition to the simple enjoyment that students may derive from talking to one another (Sandstrom & Rawn, 2015), students can also benefit from hearing about the experiences of their classmates. Hearing that others are struggling to learn just as we might be struggling to learn increases belonging and boosts achievement (Walton & Cohen, 2011; Yeager et al., 2016). As a student myself, I know I was always relieved when the people around me in a class confessed that the reading was confusing for them too or that they felt unsure about the upcoming exam.

James Lang in his 2016 book *Small Teaching* describes a variety of techniques that might lend themselves well to getting students chatting before class. For example, putting up a picture of something related to course content and listing a few questions: What do you notice? What do you wonder? Encourage students to write about what they see but also to share it with those around them prior to the start of class. In writing about techniques like this, Lang was focused on ways to motivate and engage students generally, but it seems likely that part of the reason this might work for motivation and engagement is that it gets students talking to one another. Other possibilities: post a question of the day that they are expected to discuss or play music or video clips that they can guess the age or meaning of. The idea here is just to get students talking to each other, even for brief periods, and to remember that it *does not matter* if the talk is content related. The evidence tells us that just the act of chatting is what matters.

Finally, if you are not doing so already, consider using more discussion to teach the content of the course. In a study of race-based courses that I conducted with my colleagues Nancy Chick and Terri Karis (Chick, Karis, & Kernahan, 2009), we found that courses using discussion led to greater learning and more awareness of racial privilege and institutional discrimination than a course that was lecture-based. The student participants' written responses helped us to understand why. When asked what helped them learn, many students described how important it was to hear that others were struggling just like they were. They appreciated knowing that other students were having difficult emotional reactions or trouble understanding. One common sentiment:

students (mostly White) reported feeling guilty about their own naiveté and lack of prior understanding when it came to institutional racism. Knowing that other students were similarly ignorant about institutional racism was comforting and made it easier for students to admit the ways in which their knowledge was lacking. Here we can see a simple example of how discussion in class can help students normalize their feelings, likely boosting their sense of belonging and learning as a result.

A great resource for learning more about discussion is Jay Howard's *Discussion in the College Classroom* (2015). He reviews the evidence for discussion as an effective teaching tool and provides many suggestions for how to get it going and how to use it well across a variety of teaching situations including online, small, and large-class formats.

Accept Negative Feelings and Move Beyond Them

Over the years of teaching my own course on racism, I have sometimes felt as though I unwittingly create self-help support groups. White students, feeling badly about what they are learning, confess dirty secrets about their own racism or the racism of their families and friends, and I end up worrying that we are getting off track. Because I am not a clinician, I have often felt uncomfortable when my classroom takes on this kind of confessional tone. On the one hand, I know that these feelings are normal, and I want to be accepting of my students' emotions: the guilt of White students, the anger and frustration of students of color, the hopelessness we all feel. All of these are a part of the process. But on the other hand, I want to talk about ideas and concepts and evidence. I want my students to learn about more than just their own feelings. To do this, I have come to believe, based on my teaching experiences and on what I know about the science of emotion, that we have to let students feel what they feel while *also* pushing them to move beyond themselves. Negative feelings are definitely part of the process of learning about racism, but they are not the *point* of learning about racism.

To help students move beyond just themselves, it is important to keep a few things in mind. First, remember that you are probably more experienced at this than they are. If you have been studying racism for a while, then you have probably had a lot of feelings about it. You have done the work (I hope) of thinking through your own privileges and vulnerabilities around race. As a result, you know that these feelings are normal or at least that they happen, helping you to feel less overwhelmed when you see or learn about racism. To be clear, this does not mean you do not feel angry or guilty or sad, just that you have experience and that your body knows the feelings. Remembering this helps us to be compassionate toward our students and to remember that many of them, especially if they are White, are just now doing the work that we have already done. Sometimes we need to allow space for this and our classrooms might feel temporarily uncomfortable. There might be some negativity that we need to stay with. Accepting and allowing this is usually the best way to get beyond it.

In guiding our students through these feelings, it can help to steer them toward more analysis and away from personal confession. Depending on what you are discussing or presenting, you can try asking them to think about why things are as they are. Who benefits? What are the historical factors at play? It can also be useful to ask them questions that frame privilege and advantage in more intersectional and situational terms. For example, if you want them to reflect on the concept of privilege itself, you could ask them to describe how certain parts of their own identity may advantage them while others disadvantage them. Alternatively, how does the situation they are in change their relative advantage or disadvantage? Questions like these can help students focus less on themselves and more on the larger social forces at play, a move that may help them to have more compassion for others and more of an inclination to act. When we stop making everything about ourselves and our own feelings, we often have more space to think about other people. Keeping this in mind, it is even clearer that student guilt is not a useful course objective.

Finally, when students get things wrong, when they deny course content or fail to see privilege and discrimination at play, do what you can to maintain trust. This does not mean that you do not correct obvious misunderstandings or hold them to the standards of evidence in your assignments. They still have to do the work. But you can be gentle in your correction and avoid shaming them in front of others. When I receive discussion comments or writings that challenge the premises of the content, for example, I push back in my online grading feedback. I ask for evidence and remind them that not providing it (if they are presenting unfounded claims) has lowered their score. But in class, I will often still use their comments and frame them not in terms of how wrong the student is but in terms of how common their response is. Depending on the context, I might ask the student to elaborate on their comments before asking the full class to discuss why misperceptions about race are so common. Most of the time, when students present arguments against our content, the ideas are not new but reflect larger societal myths about race. Using student comments to analyze these myths can be a great way to avoid shaming students while also sending the message that these beliefs are not supported by evidence. This process may also help students see why they have come to believe what they believe in the first place. It does not usually feel like it at the time, but students' resistant comments and questions are *helpful*. They allow us to bring up the common arguments against our content and discuss them in class in ways that emphasize both how common and also who wrong they are, without shaming anyone in the process.

—

Chapter 5

EXPECTATIONS: FROM GROUND RULES TO GROWTH MINDSETS

—

IN NOVEMBER OF 2015, as protests over racism on campus were roiling the nearby University of Missouri–Columbia campus, Andrea Quenette, a communications professor at the University of Kansas was teaching a course for graduate students on how to teach undergraduates. During the course, the issue of racism arose with Quenette telling the students, "As a white woman, I just never have seen the racism. . . ." She went on to use a racial slur, trying to make the point that it is hard for her to relate to students who may have experienced racism on campus (Jaschik, 2016). According to the students who were in the class and who later published an open letter asking that she be removed as their instructor, Quenette made several arguments that seemed to deny the existence of institutional and structural racism. In the aftermath, both Quenette and her students felt hurt, angry, and fearful. One student, interviewed later, talked about her fear of the stigma surrounding the incident. She worried that protesting her instructor might lead to the loss of her own chance at a teaching career. In March 2016, Quenette was cleared of any wrongdoing, but in May of that same year, she was told that she would not be reappointed to her tenure-track position (Flaherty, 2016).

In reading about the case, both from instructor and student perspectives, it is clear that Quenette and her students really had no clear expectations around the discussion of race. Instead, their discussion was spontaneous and unplanned, a reaction to the protests going on across the country at the time. These kinds of discussions happen, of course, and it can be great when current events provide a spark of interest and motivation, but these kinds of discussions can also be counterproductive and, in cases such as this, even harmful. In this chapter, I will try to provide some guidance around communicating expectations for your course. These will include not just expectations for class discussion, but for how students think about their learning and how they can expect their understanding to develop over the course. I will describe why expectations matter and how taking the time to think through your expectations and making them explicit and intentional can pay off later.

GROUND RULES

Brian Arao and Kristi Clemens, writing in their chapter *From Safe Spaces to Brave Spaces: A New Way to Frame Dialogue around Diversity and Social Justice*, argue that ground rules for discussion are "foundational to diversity and social justice learning activities" (p. 135, 2013). Indeed, the advice to set ground rules seems standard when it comes to teaching about race. But why? Does it help to minimize resistance?

Increase learning? It is difficult to know. Although I have seen this advice given often, I have not seen a lot of research on how or if it works. I suspect that part of the reason for this is that few teachers (myself included) want to have a "control" condition when it comes to ground rules. Many of us would balk at the notion of teaching about race without first discussing with students how we are going to do this. It feels important to set up some sort of shared expectations and rules, if for no other reason than to signal to students that we want them to participate and that we are willing to share some of our power and responsibility.

In writing about the process of setting ground rules for class, Arao and Clemens argue that it is very important to be intentional about the process, precise in your wording, and generous in the time you allot for it. They make the point that many of the shared rules that result from ground rules discussions (e.g., "agree to disagree," "no attacks," "respect") can actually get in the way of learning, conflating safety with comfort and allowing students (especially White students) to avoid grappling with difficult material. Instead, they call on instructors to consider the use of the word "brave" rather than "safe." They go on to provide some specific ways to think about how we might facilitate a ground rules discussion that pushes students toward understanding how a rule that sounds good ("agree to disagree" for example) may actually allow us to avoid engaging with evidence and stop conversations that really should continue.

Overall, I agree with much of their analysis. I think being thoughtful about our ground rules and taking the time to help students consider the implications of these rules can set a positive tone for the course. Given that motivation seems to increase when students take on more autonomy with respect to their learning, sharing in the creation of course ground rules seems like an important way to begin our semesters. As we do this, however, we also have to be mindful of how the class unfolds and how those ground rules play out in the day-to-day experiences of our students, especially our students of color.

Over the years of teaching the psychology of prejudice and racism on my mostly White campus, I have heard some comments repeatedly. One of these is the lament that there are not more people of color in class. Most often the student saying this is White and usually arguing that he or she really wants to learn more about how people of color feel, how they experience racism and stereotypes. Aside from the problem of generalizing one person's experience, there is also this: it is often the case that when a person of color *does* describe their own experiences of racial bias, they are met with disbelief or questions: "Are you sure it was about race? How do you know?" Many White people claim that they want to hear more about racism directly from those experiencing it, but then discount what they hear.

One memorable occasion of this involves an essay I have used in recent years in which an Asian man describes the stereotypes Asian men face regularly, being stereotyped as less masculine and as undesirable to women. He then connects those stereotypes to his own experiences and feelings (Cho, 2014). I typically combine this first-person account with data on interracial marriage and dating as a way to get students thinking about how racial stereotypes influence our most intimate relationships. Inevitably, though, someone will bring up the notion that the author is simply "whining" or that he just needs to have more confidence in himself. That is, the feelings the author has are not about stereotypes at all but just his own insecurity.

Listening to the students and trying to guide them back

toward the evidence and the main point, I have sometimes felt grateful that the author of the essay is not in the room. That impulse, though, does not protect the students of color who are in the room. The last time my class and I discussed this particular essay, a Black female student made the point that she often felt less attractive and that it was not enough for her to just try and "be more confident." Other women in the room, including an Asian student and several White women, nodded their heads in agreement and I reminded the students what the data show: that Asian men are less likely to marry across race and that they receive fewer contacts on online dating platforms. The evidence is clear: there are disparities in romantic opportunity and experience and these disparities are both raced and gendered. Looking back, I think that it was a useful discussion, but I also worry about the feelings of that Black female student. Why should she have to expose her own painful feelings in the service of helping a White male student understand the evidence that was before him? Experiences like this make it clear why students of color can feel targeted and angry in courses about racism and why they may feel the need to resist via withdrawal as a way to self-protect.

It is just this kind of situation that I believe the columnist Lily Zheng is referring to in her 2016 Stanford Daily opinion piece "Why your Brave Space Sucks." Specifically, she argues that marginalized people, including people of color, often do the work of educating those with more privilege and power. Taking issue with the idea that students need to be braver and talking back specifically to Arao and Clemens (the authors of the chapter I cited earlier), Zheng says, "If privileged people are gaining knowledge at the expense of marginalized peoples' well-being, then your brave space sucks." Reading these words, I was reminded of the findings of various studies showing how White students may benefit more from classes on diversity than students of color (Bowman, 2009) and how White people in general experience more positive effects from interracial contact as compared to people of color (Tropp & Page-Gould, 2015). Across a variety of inter-racial situations, it is often the case that White people learn more and feel better when compared to their racial minority peers, often because people of color are helping White people to "catch up" in terms of racial understanding and serving as examples for how these processes work.

As an instructor, I do not know of a perfect set of ground rules and, to be honest, I do not really believe that perfec-tion is even possible (more on that later). Instead, I think we have to take the evidence we have and keep it in mind as we design and run our courses. We know that White students and students of color are going to experience our classes differently and that their resistance to course material may vary as a result. You may recall from Chapter 2 that students of color often resist in more passive and self-pro-tective ways and they may feel more anger, whereas White students may be more active and outspoken and feel more guilt. Knowing this, we can attempt to minimize resistance generally through increased belonging, affirmation, and the other techniques described throughout this book. But we should also be especially vigilant when it comes to the students who are most vulnerable in the room, usually our students of color. We can watch for early signs of withdrawal and intervene privately when needed to ensure a student feels cared for and seen. In a more preventive fashion, and as described more fully back in Chapter 2, I often try to talk privately with students of color early in the term, or contact them by email, to affirm their experience and let them know that I know that they have experiences with racism that I

and their White classmates have not had. I also let them
know that it is not their responsibility to speak for their
race or share their experiences if they do not want to. It
really is up to them. I also never call on anyone to share their
experiences unless they have shared these experiences first
in an online discussion posting. It is unrealistic to think
that every discussion will feel safe to all students, but if our
students feel that they can trust us, that we are keeping
an eye on things and that we understand that they may be
feeling targeted, they may be more willing to engage with
the classrooms that we are asking them to co-create.

WARNINGS

At the same time that you are creating ground rules, it may
also be useful to warn students about what they can expect
from your course. As a young instructor, I first encountered
the idea of warnings from the incomparable Beverly Daniel
Tatum. In my first semester of teaching about racism and
prejudice (fall 1999), I was surprised and befuddled by the
resistance I faced. I realize now how naïve I was, but at the
time, it was difficult to imagine that students would push
back on the information I was providing. They certainly were
not doing that in my introductory psychology courses! The
force of their emotional reactions, their sadness and guilt
as well as their anger surprised me. Searching for answers, I
emailed Dr. Tatum (then teaching at Mount Holyoke College)
out of desperation. Two years before, she had published the
important book *Why Are All the Black Kids Sitting Together in
the Cafeteria?* She kindly emailed me back and even sent me
a copy of her syllabus. She also pointed me toward her published work examining how students learn in courses about
race (Tatum, 1992; 1994). This helped me immeasurably,

not only providing me with some concrete answers about teaching, but also showing me a new way to think about scholarship in terms of teaching and learning.

One of her concrete suggestions and something that was included in her syllabus was a set of warnings for her students. The listing was straightforward, telling students that they might expect to have any number of emotional responses including anger and sadness and that they might feel the need to distance themselves from the material at some point, tuning out or withdrawing. She emphasized these experiences as normal and further tells students that those in earlier classes were able to move beyond their feelings and succeed in class. In her 1992 article, Tatum argues that warnings like these are essential for student learning and she provides evidence from her course comments. In a moment, I will describe how I have replicated those findings in my own work and discuss how you might use warnings in your own courses, but first I want to acknowledge how warnings have taken on a different meaning in recent years.

If you want to start an interesting conversation at your next faculty meeting or just enliven any gathering of instructors, try bringing up the idea of trigger warnings. Next to laptop bans and declining state support, trigger warnings are sure to generate strong feelings and righteous opinions. But despite the caricatures of "snowflake" students and overly careful professors, research on this topic suggests a more nuanced picture. According to Guy Boysen, who published an excellent review of trigger warnings in 2017, trigger warnings actually refer to a very specific kind of warning: "Prior notification of an educational topic so that students may prepare for or avoid distress that is automatically evoked by that topic due to clinical mental health problems" (p. 164). The National Coalition against Censorship

(NCAC) defined trigger warnings a bit more generally for their 2015 survey as "written warnings to alert students in advance that material assigned in a course might be upsetting or offensive" (p. 3). Even when defined without reference to clinical mental health problems, NCAC found that there were not large numbers of students clamoring for these warnings (about 15 percent of the instructors they surveyed reported that students had requested warnings) and that less than 1 percent of campuses had formal policies requiring trigger warnings. In terms of instructor usage, 23 percent reported using content warnings regularly, but these instructors drew a distinction between flagging specific pieces of content (which they were not doing) and instead providing detailed descriptions of the course content in the syllabus as a way to let students know what to expect. In other words, they were drawing a distinction between trigger warnings and the more general practice of informing students about the course.

It is this latter idea that better fits what Tatum describes and what I myself do in class. Moreover, I do not (and generally would not; see below for some exceptions) allow students to avoid content. Just because something is upsetting does not mean students can avoid it. My main thesis throughout this book has been that what we teach is rightly and necessarily difficult. Rather than avoiding that difficulty, I would argue that we have to accept it and accept that our students will struggle as they learn. By letting students know how they might feel as they learn, the goal is to help students see that their reactions are normal and just another part of the learning process.

To understand the kinds of warnings I give and to see how they may influence student learning, I would again cite the study I conducted with colleagues (Chick, Karis & Kernahan,

2009) as well as that earlier work by Tatum (1992). In our own study of four diversity-based courses, my colleagues and I not only worked with our students to set ground rules for discussion, but we also gave our students information about what they might expect in terms of their own emotional responses and how the learning process typically unfolds for students. Tatum found in her classes that this kind of pre-course warning was useful, especially in terms of helping students to see that their responses were normative and at least somewhat predictable. Our larger study essentially replicated her earlier findings and extended them to other kinds of courses. We found that many students noted the warnings and introductory information as especially useful in helping them learn. As we wrote at the time, "those who knew what to expect emotionally and those who learned that other classmates were having similar emotional experiences were more likely to stay with the learning process and grapple with new information, even when it generated uncomfortable feelings" (p. 11). These findings not only suggest the importance of warnings, but they also provide yet more evidence for the key role of discussion; our respondents noted hearing the experiences and difficulties of fellow classmates multiple times as an especially important aid in their learning.

Over the years, I have had a few different versions of course warnings, but all have essentially contained the same information. Here is my most current version (listed as part of the syllabus):

1. You may feel anger, resentment, guilt, sadness, tension, and helplessness as you learn. This is normal and will ebb and flow as you learn. Try to push yourself to keep learning, even when things feel upsetting or confusing.

2. We will rely on social science for the facts of the course, but your feelings are your own and you can express them.
3. Everyone's experiences are different depending on their circumstances and the context. This difference creates differences in attitude that can then be considered with respect to the larger body of evidence.
4. Most students learn and enjoy the process of learning in this class.
5. It is not expected that you will do or say things perfectly (myself included), but we can all work towards learning.

See Tatum (1992) for another description of both the course warning and the course ground rules and assumptions that she used over her years of teaching the psychology of racism. See also Chick et al. (2009) for a longer description of the warnings and information we provided to students as part of our larger study.

One last point before moving on from warnings: there may be specific times when students are simply too upset to meaningfully engage with a specific piece of content. In my experience, this is generally not about resistance to learning but instead has more to do with the vividness of description. For example, students who are veterans of war can experience upsetting reactions in response to vivid descriptions or scenes of violence, survivors of sexual assault may be unable to read vivid descriptions of assault, and students of color may likewise have strong reactions to vivid depictions of racist violence. This will not be the case for all students, but it is a possibility. For this reason, it is important to keep an open mind and open channels of communication with students, letting them know that their feelings and reactions are important and that they can come to us with concerns if needed. Once or twice in my long teaching career I have found alternatives for my students to read or to watch (in the case of a video presentation) if their emotional reaction was just too strong for them to meaningfully benefit. In a more preventative fashion, it is good practice in a course about racism to try and consider our content from the perspective of our students of color. For example, vivid video depictions of slavery or racial violence shown in class might be especially difficult, giving students of color little time to process their feelings and making them feel more in the spotlight, something that we know they likely already feel if they are one of only a few students of color in the class (Crosby et al., 2014). A better approach might be to avoid especially graphic depictions in class, saving them for out-of-class viewing or reading and then discussing them in class.

POWER IN THE COURSE

Returning for a moment to the idea of ground rules, I want to highlight a suggestion that is often paired with the setting of these rules: sharing this work with our students (Aaro & Clemens, 2013). Co-creating these rules with our students, the thinking goes, will ensure that all of us, instructors and students, feel some responsibility for abiding by the rules we have made. In addition to engendering greater buy-in, we may also be signaling to our students that we are willing to share our power with them. As noted elsewhere in this book, we as instructors hold much of the power in our classrooms. We set the agenda, make the demands, and determine what work will be done and how it will be assessed. We also largely set the tone for our classrooms. Students determine their own engagement and participation, but they are still largely reacting to the terms and conditions we have set. What can we learn from the teaching literature to help us use our power well? How can we avoid unforced errors in courses that are already likely to heighten students' fears of coercion?

First, being fair is important. As multiple authors have noted (Cavanagh, 2016; Goodboy, 2011; Seidel & Tanner, 2013), unfairness is one of the most common precursors of student resistance, dissent, and negative feeling toward an instructor. Perceptions that we are grading in subjective ways, that we favor some students or viewpoints over others, or that we have unfair assignments and procedures can all increase the chances of resistance. One way to decrease these perceptions is to be as explicit as possible in terms of why you are doing what you are doing and what steps you are taking to make grading as fair and objective as possible (Seidel & Turner, 2013). Echoing this idea, Cavanagh (2016) advises the use of clear rubrics and a clear focus on how student efforts (not viewpoints or other individual characteristics) can result in higher grades. Finally, providing students with mechanisms through which they can voice their concerns and being available to hear those concerns can go a long way toward easing perceptions that you are unfair in your treatment of students. One nice way to do this might be the use of a midterm check-in—an evaluation of the course midway through that allows students to anonymously voice their concerns and see you respond to them. Stephen Brookfield (2015) lays out a relatively simple process for doing this via his Critical Incident Questionnaire. You can find that questionnaire and the instructions for its use online and in several of his books. There are other models for doing this (see Angelo & Cross, 1993, for a variety of assessment suggestions), so you may want to look around a bit to find what fits, but the real point is to communicate to students that you care about their experience and that you will work to improve it where possible.

In addition to fairness and the perception of fairness, it also pays to keep an eye on the kinds of behavior that are upsetting to students and may trigger dissent. In one study, cited by Seidel and Tanner (2013), students listed particular behaviors that they felt were aversive and upsetting. Sarcasm and put-downs, being late or absent without notice, straying from the topic, and being unresponsive to student issues were all highly ranked as "instructor misbehaviors." A similar study (Goodboy, 2011) found that after unfairness, "instructor offensiveness" was a strong contributor to feelings of dissent and resistance. This category included things like violating the syllabus and being "lazy" (not providing timely feedback, for example). Taken together, an old-fashioned prescription presents itself: being kind and sensitive to the needs of our students, doing what we say we will do, and being clear about our policies and procedures. Although this is likely good practice for every class, it is especially important when we are teaching about race.

One final note on power: all of this is much more difficult for instructors who represent marginalized identities (people of color, women, graduate students, contingent or adjunct instructors). I described this back in Chapter 3 in the context of teaching evaluations, but it bears repeating here. Women and people of color often receive lower teaching evaluations. These groups are also more likely to have their credentials questioned and their authority tested (Sue et al., 2011). Just to add another degree of difficulty, instructors of color are also more likely to be perceived as "self-interested" when it comes to discussing race, thus lowering an already lower credibility in the eyes of some students (Crittle & Maddox, 2017). What this means, of course, is that despite being kind and responsive, you are still more likely to face resistance as an instructor if you represent one of these groups. It is important for those in administration as well as those in the faculty ranks to understand these challenges and to avoid over-interpreting teaching evaluations or student complaints when evaluating faculty of color, particularly when those faculty are teaching courses on race.

ROLES AND STRUCTURE

Have you ever noticed how quickly things shift when you see your students outside of a school context? Seeing a student at the gym, at the store, or any other off-campus space always reminds me that I am not nearly as comfortable with my students as I might believe. I think this happens, at least in part, because the classroom is a very structured space. Our roles are clear and defined and, as the instructor, I am the one in charge. It can be easy to forget this. Those of us who think of ourselves as warm and funny in the classroom can feel confused when our students are not as warm toward us outside of the classroom or perhaps our jokes are not as funny. We fail to account for how the context has changed: we are no longer within our more powerful and structured roles, we are not ensconced in the expectations of the typical classroom. Consider this: do you expect a classroom to be a space where you will laugh a lot? Probably not. This is why even the smallest joke in a classroom might seem hilarious. Outside of class, in a more relaxed space, the same joke is less likely to feel funny. The material might be the same, but the context is different.

The good news is that, despite our occasional discomfort outside of class, within the classroom we can use the power of roles and structure to help students engage and participate more comfortably. To see this, it helps to know a little more about what psychologists have found with respect to structure and roles and interracial discussions. First, interracial discussions are a great petri dish for understanding difficult discussions more generally. Typically, cross-race discussions provoke anxiety, in Whites as well as in people of color, and this anxiety is heightened when the topic of discussion is race itself (Tropp & Page-Gould, 2015). Experimental research, however, has found that structuring interracial interactions lessens anxiety and improves performance when compared to more free-form interactions (Avery, Richeson, Hebl, & Ambady, 2009; Babbitt & Sommers, 2011; Toosi, Babbitt, Ambady, & Sommers, 2012). In other words, when you ask people to focus on a specific task or give them scripts to follow, you tend to get better results and less discomfort. This makes intuitive sense I think. Imagine being told that you will be meeting someone who is new to teaching on your campus, finding out that this person is of a different race from you, and then being told, "Please talk about diversity." Compare that to the same situation, but this time you are asked, "Please list some examples of how race and diversity can create difficult moments in the classroom." The former is wide open. Should you discuss work? Pop culture? Politics? The latter is specific and actionable. Even better, it capitalizes on something that both of you presumably know something about. Research has found, not surprisingly, that the latter is much less likely to provoke anxiety or concern about being seen as racially biased (if you are White) or being the victim of racial bias (if you are a person of color). You have a script to follow.

Translating this to the classroom, there have been studies examining how particular roles or structured assignments may increase learning. For example, Parrott and Cherry (2011) outlined a role-based discussion technique that assigns students to rotating discussion group roles (e.g., leader, passage master, devil's advocate) within the same small group throughout the semester. The students receive points for completing reading prep sheets prior to coming to class and for contributions made during class discussions. Within their small groups, students have assigned roles and specific instructions for discussion. In assessing this technique across several courses, the authors found that students were not only very positive about the technique, but that they were more likely to prepare for class and complete their readings. Another theme in their findings showed that students understood the material better with many commenting on how their roles helped them to see a variety of different perspectives on the readings.

Taken together, these findings—along with findings from other, similar kinds of teaching methods (e.g., Interteaching) and the more general findings for structured interactions—suggest that giving our students particular roles to play can lead to a more positive and productive classroom atmosphere. This may be particularly the case for courses that focus on race. Talking about race, even with same-race peers, may increase anxiety and fear. Students, at least in my courses and those of my colleagues, often report worries over misperceptions and the possibility that they will say the wrong thing. Creating structures for participation through clear tasks and roles may help to alleviate these anxieties and increase understanding.

EXPECTATIONS OF GROWTH AND CHANGE

In 2012, the writer Lesley Kinzel devoted a blog post in the (now defunct) *XO Jane* online magazine to answering the question: "How do I stop accidentally offending people all the time?" The reader who submitted the question confessed to having just offended two people that very morning because of her own racial and cultural insensitivity. She felt unclear about what might be offensive and what was not and wanted some guidance. In response, Kinzel wrote that the questioner should first "give up" on the idea of not offending people. That by virtue of living in a social world and interacting with other people, offense is going to happen. We are going to mess up and make mistakes; we should expect it to happen. She goes on to argue that when these offenses occur, it is up to us to learn from them and to figure out how to make changes going forward. Inherent in this idea is the notion that people can grow and change, that we can get better at understanding how biases manifest themselves and that we can become kinder and more compassionate while never being "perfect."

If you are a parent or if you have been paying attention to the teaching and learning literature in the last decade or so, you have likely heard about growth mindset (see the Mindset Scholars Network at mindsetscholarsnetwork.org for more information and a great overview). Lesley Kinzel does not frame her answer to the questioner in terms of growth mindset, but it is really the same basic notion: understanding that you are capable of growth and change and that this attitude, rather than a more fixed mindset, is the way to help yourself actually grow and change.

This idea is well established within the social psychological literature. Researchers know that there is a continuum of belief around how easily things like personality and intelligence can change (Schumann & Dweck, 2014). Our "implicit theories" about ourselves and other people range from "entity" or fixed beliefs on one side to "incrementalism" or growth beliefs on the other. Although many Americans lean more towards the fixed side of that continuum, particularly with respect to intelligence, a lot of research has shown that having a growth mindset is beneficial. Luckily, research has also shown that growth mindsets can be induced, helping people to improve themselves, learn more, and even improve their relationships with others. Here, I want to show how we might use this idea to improve our courses and to help students understand that they are capable of understanding and talking about race more effectively. To do that, we need to take a quick detour to examine more closely how growth mindsets can help us to improve our relationships.

What do you do when you are in trouble with a partner or spouse? When you know you have made a mistake or that the anger you so self-righteously held a few hours ago was way, way off? If you are anything like most people, you probably try to find a way to justify those feelings. As you might remember from our discussion about resistance, we often feel cognitive dissonance when what we do or think (I am part of a racist system, I have racially biased thoughts and have done racist things) is at odds with how we like to think of ourselves (I am a good person). This works in a similar way in interpersonal relationships. We like to think of ourselves as basically good, so when we do things that are not so good (getting overly angry, snapping, lying, etc.) we often try to find ways to justify that behavior to reduce any cognitive dissonance (I was busy or stressed, they hurt or harmed me first). In other words, we change the meaning of our bad behavior so that it is not as much of a threat to our view of ourselves as generally good people (see Tavris & Aronson, 2015, for an excellent review of how we justify our behavior across lots of situations).

The problem here, of course, is that when you rationalize away your misdeeds, your partner is likely to become even angrier. We have all received the "non-apology apology" where someone tells us that they are sorry but that they were just tired or stressed or . . . blah, blah. Not surprisingly, this does not really work very well. What does work, however, is actually taking responsibility with no excuses. Research has found that fully taking responsibility for what we have done decreases anger and improves positive feelings in relationships. So, what stops us? Again, it is that annoying feeling of cognitive dissonance. Taking responsibility would mean accepting a view of ourselves that is threatening or uncomfortable and this threat undermines our willingness to take responsibility and apologize without justification.

In researching how and when people take responsibility for their transgressions in close relationships, Schumann and Dweck (2014) decided to take a closer look at the role that mindset can play. They hypothesized that those with a growth mindset might be more willing to accept responsibility for their actions, thus making their apologies better. Across a series of four different studies, this is exactly what they found. Interestingly, they also found that those who were willing to accept more responsibility felt less threat (as compared to those with more fixed mindsets) and that they had a greater motivation to learn about themselves and their relationship in the context of their transgressions. In other words, people who believe that personality is changeable understand that they can learn and grow from their mistakes. As a result, they are more willing to think about their transgressions and learn from them. On the other side, those who believe that personality is fixed seem to find themselves more stuck. It makes sense; if I believe that personality is fixed, any flaws I find are going to stick around and continue to be a problem (how can I change them?) and so I am then less motivated to believe that they are truly flaws. I do not want to accept responsibility or talk about them. I opt instead to justify my actions, further damaging my relationship. One last hopeful point from this study: the researchers found that they could *induce* a growth mindset with respect to personality. That is, they were able to help their participants see personality differently, even if that was not their go-to mindset, and that change led the participants to take more responsibility for transgressions, ultimately improving their relationships.

Translating these ideas back to the classroom suggests that we will want to emphasize a growth mindset with our students as a way to help them avoid the dissonance reduction trap. For many students, understanding the scope and size of racism is both overwhelming and personally implicating. For White students, the understanding that racism creates a kind of privilege that benefits them every day in ways seen and unseen comes into conflict with the belief that they are good people. Not racist people. Racism is also deeply threatening to the idea of meritocracy, that one's own effort and hard work are the main reason for one's success. For students of color, the burden is different, but dissonance is still present. A pervasive and institutionally based racism is both angering and disempowering, making it difficult to feel in control of one's own future. To help our students accept what they are learning and better understand the mistakes that they may make as they try to live within this system of race and racism, a growth mindset is beneficial.

Students need to know that they are going to make mistakes, that no one understands these issues perfectly, and that they are capable of change and growth. One way I have done this is to use myself as an example. I often describe how, despite my knowledge of race, stereotypes still pop into my thinking and how I try to catch them in the moment. I also talk about my own fears of saying the "wrong thing" when I talk to other people, especially the people of color I work with and other professors who study race. I let them know that I worry about getting it right. Finally, I sometimes describe my own research with previous classes showing that students became more comfortable with the idea of acting on racism or talking about race only *after* they have finished the course or even up to a year later (Kernahan & Davis, 2007; 2010). The idea is to send two messages: 1) everyone struggles, even an expert, and 2) previous students struggled but they were able to grow and change into new understandings.

To date, I have not done any classroom research on growth mindsets and learning about race, but other, more general research on teaching and learning has been very strong. For example, incorporating growth messages into student feedback (Cohen, Steele, & Ross, 1999; Yeager et al., 2014) and into college orientation materials (Yeager et al., 2016) has been shown to improve performance, increase the likelihood that students will revise their work, and increase retention. By helping our students to see themselves as capable of growth and change and emphasizing that that this is an ongoing process, we may lessen our students' feelings of threat and motivate them to learn.

SELF-EFFICACY AND EMPOWERMENT

One final expectation that may be useful in teaching about race involves empowering your students. Specifically, and depending on your content and goals, you may want to help students see that they are not only capable of learning and changing, but also that they can take anti-racist action if they so choose. Multiple research findings point toward the

importance of this strategy, including a review of the literature of diversity initiatives conducted by Moss-Racusin et al.
(2014). These researchers found that empowerment was one
of the key elements necessary for the success of any training
aimed at improving diversity and reducing bias. Trainings
that stressed a shared responsibility for social oppression
and a shared ability to work towards mitigating bias and
discrimination were the most likely to work (they also noted
the importance of active engagement and the importance of
avoiding blame). Another way of thinking about this is that
those programs that helped their participants to see their
own role in solving social problems were more successful and
faced less backlash and resistance.

A nice example of this approach, assessed with undergraduates, is the WAGES intervention for everyday sexism. Social
psychologists designed WAGES to promote self-efficacy
and to reduce reactance to learning about sexism (Cundiff,
Zawadzki, Danube, & Shields, 2014). The WAGES (Workshop
Activity for Gender Equity Simulation) intervention works
like a game. Participants, working in teams, simulate the
experience of trying to move up in the workplace. One
team experiences the subtle and everyday sexist biases that
women often face, and one team does not. A facilitator works
with the groups to help them see how their differential experiences connect to the real workplaces of men and women
and how they might use their understanding to see everyday
sexism more clearly.

Results showed that the intervention increases perceptions of the harms of everyday sexism. They also showed
that decreased defensiveness is part of what drives that
increased understanding of everyday sexism. Another
driver? Increased feelings of self-efficacy. In other words,
the students who participated in the game (both men and

women) felt surer that they could recognize and overcome everyday sexism. Seeing that they were capable in this way helped them to be less defensive and more open to learning. By contrast, the "information-only" condition (no game) did not improve perceptions of everyday sexism or feelings of empowerment. When students simply learned about sexism without participating in an activity and discussion, they were less likely to see everyday sexism as harmful. They were also more likely to believe that the information was exaggerated. When only given the information, and not the chance to experience it more actively, both men and women got defensive. To get real understanding and to get beyond resistance, the authors had to engage the participants and help them to see their own role in things. As instructors, we can apply these findings to our classrooms, designing activities and delivering content in ways that are active and allow for self-relevance and empowerment.

In my own teaching, I have tried to incorporate empowerment through a writing and presentation assignment that I stumbled upon thanks to Beverly Daniel Tatum. You may recall my desperate email to her and her gracious response during my difficult first semester of teaching about race. At that point, I could not get my students to believe the content, let alone feel empowered to do something about it. Included in the syllabus and readings she sent was the idea of assigning students an "action paper." That is, asking students to write about how they will take action themselves as part of the final assignment of the course. I have now done some version of this paper, including a presentation in addition to the written assignment, multiple times. In short, the assignment asks students to consider the following questions: Do you want to take anti-racist action? If so, what do you want to do and why do you think it will work?

If you do not want to act, please explain why you do not? Whatever they choose, the students have to provide evidence for their choices, and I try to be flexible with respect to sources. Just a side-note: as of this writing, no one has argued for taking no action at all. Instead, most students focus on starting with themselves, listing specific areas that they hope to learn more about and the ways in which their learning can help them do a better job as employees or parents. A shorter version of this assignment simply asks students what they are most interested in learning more about and why. They then provide evidence for the importance of their learning and give a listing of the books, films, podcasts, blogs, and so on that they plan to consume along with descriptions of what makes each a good source. Either way, you can ask them to deliver their answers via paper, presentation, or both. Anecdotally, many students have told me or commented in evaluations that they appreciate this opportunity to end the course in a hopeful way and to relate their learning back to themselves and their own ability to do something about racism, even if that something is simply to learn more at this point.

SUMMARIZED RECOMMENDATIONS AND SUGGESTIONS

Set Up Ground Rules for the Course

As part of a first- or second-day activity, consider discussing course discussion itself. How should it work? What are the rules everyone should follow? Often, it can be useful to do this after asking the students to write a little bit about their expectations for the course: What they are excited about? What they are fearful about? Given what we know about power in the classroom, the idea here is to try and share

some of that power, allowing students a say and some responsibility for how the course will feel and proceed.

At the same time, it is important to use this rule-making
process as a way to help students see that not all the rules
they propose are going to be appropriate for learning in your
course (Arao & Clemens, 2013). For example, a common pro-
posal from students is "agreeing to disagree." On first listen,
this sounds good and fair, but the truth is that there are
likely to be several points in class that are not up for debate
or disagreement. You would never want students to "agree to
disagree" about the realities of racism itself. For this reason,
it is important to be mindful during this process of how
the rules that are developed will affect learning. Specially,
will the rules let them stop learning when things are uncomfortable, or will they push them towards using evidence
and expertise to resolve disagreements? Helping students
to consider these ideas early in the course can be a good
preventive measure away from feel-good but useless rules
of discussion that reinforce the idea that all racial groups
are equal or equally victimized by the system of racism we
inhabit.

Another consideration of the rule-making process is
the privacy and protection of students. In my experience,
students will often propose that what they say should not
be repeated outside of the course and that, in general, they
should respect one another enough to allow for mistakes in
what they say. I like to reinforce these ideas or nudge them in
that direction if they need it. As noted earlier, it is important
to set expectations of growth and change. They should not
be expected to be perfect or to get it right all the time. It is
a class, after all, and they are there to learn. Emphasizing
the importance of giving each other the space to learn and
grow can help make the class a more compassionate space

at the same time that it helps students to develop more of a growth mindset around learning about race.

Finally, do the rules allow for the protection of those who are most vulnerable in the room? Marginalized students should be reassured that if they share their experiences, their feelings and their pain will not be dismissed or minimized. Such rules are often articulated by students in abstract ways such as "respecting others." You can then nudge them towards more specifics, helping them to drill down on what respect looks like in practice. That sharing a particular experience can be difficult and it is important to listen without judging immediately. In addition, I often make a distinction between respecting each individual's experiences and understanding the role of evidence in generalizing about racism. The importance of this distinction comes up repeatedly as the courses progresses, so I find it useful to have a talking point in place that can be returned to. To wrap up, I often snap a picture of the rules we have co-created (written on the board usually, but you could also type them up) and post them to the course's online space or website.

One final suggestion on the discussion about discussion. Jay Howard, in his 2015 book *Discussion in the College Classroom* (2015), suggests asking students to think a little bit about how they like to participate. Do they generally like to think by thinking first and then talking or do they prefer to think as they talk? Do they want to raise their hands to speak or "just talk" as part of a freer flowing discussion? There are often students who feel more comfortable holding back, thinking first and raising their hands to join in, while others like to think by talking and want to just jump in. I like students to see that there are differences in style and I often encourage them to try out ways of participating that are different from their own. I also emphasize that their style may shift over the course of the semester as they get more comfortable (something I have seen often). The point is to develop an early sense of each other and an expectation of growth and change with respect to participation.

Consider Warnings

Scholarship of teaching and learning research has shown that warnings can be a useful way to help students learn (Chick et al., 2009; Tatum, 1992). Here I am not talking about the much maligned and misunderstood notion of "trigger warnings." In fact, the research does not suggest that each piece of potentially upsetting content you provide should be flagged or that students should be able to avoid particular readings because they are difficult. Instead, the idea is just to let students know upfront that the general content of the course may be difficult for them emotionally. My own research suggests that doing so provides a meta-affective strategy that students can use to help them better understand their own feelings and see them as part of the normal learning process (Chick et al., 2009). In this way warnings do not shield students from learning but invite them into the process in an informed way.

There are multiple ways to offer warnings. As I noted earlier in the chapter, I like to list my own warnings in the syllabus as a set of expectations for class. Tatum (1992) reports doing something very similar, and you can see the text of her written warnings there. Other instructors might be more comfortable offering the warnings verbally. In their study of abnormal psychology courses, Boysen, Wells, and

Dawson (2016) wanted to know how instructors handled warnings about course content given the references in that particular course to trauma, suicide, and other distressing topics. What they found was that about half of instructors offered warnings of some type, with most doing so verbally throughout the semester (72 percent). Smaller numbers reported giving warnings in the syllabus (37 percent), in particular assignments (21 percent), or in the course learning management system (10 percent). Depending on your content, you may want to warn generally about the course (as I do) or more specifically about upcoming topics (as found in this study).

A final way to think about warnings is to consider the content from the perspective of your students of color and, if necessary, provide them a specific warning. If you show videos or require readings that are especially vivid in their depictions of racist violence (e.g., lynching, whipping of enslaved people), remember that these depictions could be especially difficult for students of color to process in a classroom surrounded by mostly White students. Considering this, it might be better to ask students to view or read these materials outside of class as a way to alleviate unnecessary anxiety. If they have to be shown or read in class, consider letting the class know that some parts could be tough to watch or listen to and perhaps provide a general description before you get started. Another way to think about this is to provide a general warning for students of color as part of a broader communication you send early in the semester. At that point, you can let students of color in your class know that there may be upsetting content along the way, but that you do not expect them to be a representative for their race in response to any of the material in the course, that their reaction is their own.

Think About Power in the Classroom

Everything we do in the classroom is affected and influenced by the power we carry as instructors. It is very easy to forget this, especially since we often feel vulnerable as we teach, wondering if our students like what we are doing, if the course is working, if it is rigorous enough, and so on. Based on the evidence covered earlier, however, it is clear that power plays an important role in how our students perceive us and in how much they are willing to engage in our courses. To use our power well, research suggests, really boils down to a few basic things: being fair, being clear, and being thoughtful about student needs.

One important place to check in on your use of power is in your feedback and grading processes. Are they relatively transparent? Are you providing enough feedback to help students improve? Although I used to greatly dislike rubrics, in recent years I have come around to their use, largely because they can speed up the grading process for written work and also because they provide students with a standardized and "objective" set of criteria that have the potential to decrease perceptions of unfairness or murkiness around grading (Stevens & Levi, 2012). I have also begun to experiment with recording my feedback in audio files rather than writing or typing it. Again, this saves time, but it also allows students to hear my voice and to (hopefully) better understand my meaning as I deliver both critiques and praise. Whatever tools and processes you use, the key thing is honesty about how students will feel in response and perhaps getting some feedback from them as a way to improve and provide better guidance. Letting our students know that we care about their feelings, that we believe they can improve and that they can use our feedback to do so, can be a potent motivator and a use of power that increases trust rather than decreasing it (Yeager et al., 2014).

Consider Providing Roles for Discussion

Over the years I have taught about racism, it is obvious to me that while many students are genuinely interested in the topic and want to know more, most are pretty anxious about it. You have likely seen that too. White students worry about being seen as racist; students marginalized by race worry about being tokenized, stereotyped, and disbelieved when they share their experiences. Openly acknowledging such feelings as part of the aforementioned "discussion about discussion" while also providing classroom practices and policies that help to script interactions and provide structure can help students participate more freely. It may seem incongruous, but providing structure seems to signal safety for students, allowing them to be part of the discussion and to learn more.

Two specific examples of structured discussion are the structured reading groups method described by Parrott and Cherry (2011) and Inter-teaching, a method that was recently systematically reviewed (Sturmey, Dalfen, and Fienup, 2015). Both methods share some similarities in that they ask students to complete the reading ahead of time and tie incentives to that work, awarding points for the ahead-of-time work as well as for the in-class participation that is done as part of an established team. In the case of structured reading groups, students are assigned a very specific role to play (and these roles rotate) that guides how they respond to the reading as well as what their contribution to the in-class discussion should be (e.g., summarizer, devil's advocate, etc.). In the case of Inter-teaching, students all complete a similar "prep guide" as they read and then discuss within small groups using those prep guides. Both methods combine small-group discussion with larger, whole-class follow-ups (typically), allowing the instructor to correct misconceptions, answer questions, and provide further elaboration where needed. Overall, studies of these methods have shown mostly positive results with increased course enjoyment, learning, and reading compliance. Additionally, methods like this can provide students with the guidance for participation they need when discussing racism.

Set the Expectation for Struggle and for Overcoming That Struggle

One of the problems with teaching about race, part of what makes people so hesitant to participate in learning about it, is the fear of saying the wrong thing. This seems especially true for White people, but everyone can struggle with this, particularly in racially diverse contexts. Luckily for us, a college classroom is a space that is supposed to be about learning, a place that can allow for mistakes and growth. Because of this, we can emphasize to our students over and over again that they are not expected to be perfect when it comes to talking about or understanding racism. The message is simple: everyone struggles with learning and thinking about race, no one says the right things all the time, and most people get more comfortable over time if they keep doing it. As I noted earlier, this message is a type of growth mindset in contrast to the more fixed way of thinking most Americans carry when it comes to understanding a variety of personal characteristics (intelligence, personality). This message of growth and the expectations you set around struggle and not being perfect when it comes to talking about race can be embedded in the warnings you provide to students (see my own example earlier in this chapter and Tatum, 1992) as well as in the ground rules you co-create with students. However you do this, the point is to empower students to see themselves as people working to overcome the normal challenges and difficulties associated with learning about race and engaging in anti-racist behavior. As noted earlier, such empowerment is probably essential to helping students engage with the material.

Chapter 6

—

COURSE CONTENT: PROBLEMS AND SOLUTIONS

—

EACH TIME I HAVE TAUGHT about race and racism there seems to come a moment when I get some variation on the following question, always from a White student: "When will we learn more about how White people have been mistreated?" It typically happens a few weeks into the semester, but occasionally this question seems to linger in the mind of a student for the entirety of the course. A few years back, I got this in my written evaluations:

> Dr. Kernahan would often say "that is what the statistics say" in terms of how racism is demonstrated throughout society. However, these statistics are coming from places like NPR, *New York Times*, etc., which are liberal. Why not any other sources used that are more fair and balanced, like Fox News?

Reading this was upsetting, but not surprising. The idea that we ought to have "balance" in what we provide to our students to give the perspective of "both sides" seems to be a common refrain. Not only do I hear it almost every time

I teach, but I have found that those who teach other controversial topics hear it too (e.g., climate change, evolution, GMOs, gender and sexism).

Usually, when I hear this question I try to deliver the news (there is no other side) in a way that acknowledges how important the question is. Because it is important. As noted back in Chapter 1, expertise on race means that there is a big gap between what we understand and what our students understand. For most Americans, racism is about individual acts of unkind behavior. For others, especially those who study race, racism is about White supremacy: systemic and systematic unearned advantage for White people and systemic and systematic disadvantage for people of color. In asking this question, students are really hitting on the key thing that they will need to learn to begin to understand how race and racism work. There are not two sides. We are not a nation of relatively equal racial groups striving for the opportunities afforded to anyone who plays by the colorblind rules. Instead, we are a nation of unequal groups with unequal levels of power, rooted in a history and culture of White supremacy. It just is not as simple as "two sides." I try to be upfront about this with students, pointing out that there is no evidence I can provide them that will tell them otherwise. No good evidence, anyway, and this is really the main point: there are standards for what counts as evidence and it is important to use those standards, just as any expert in any field would.

This is a simple message, but it is not an easy lesson. The questioning of content typically comes up multiple times and in various ways. I have had students tell me that they "hate" the textbook authors or that the author must be an "angry Black man" (in reference to a White sociologist). I have had students tell me that what I am giving them certainly "cannot be true" or that if it were true they would have heard this before now. On and on and in various ways. Because I know that learning often works this way, moving forward only to fall back, I try to remind myself to be patient and to remember that this is part of the process. But again, this is not easy. In this chapter I will try to provide examples and information to help illuminate why this process can be so difficult as well as ideas for making it better. Specifically, I'll provide a bit more information on disagreements around content and what they may really be about, the inclusion of all racialized groups, Whiteness and White privilege in a course on race, and some evidence-based methods for content delivery.

One quick note before beginning. The topic of this chapter, content, may feel limited. There are many things to learn beyond content knowledge, including important skills like information literacy, thinking critically, writing, working with others, and so on, and I do not want to discount those skills or imply that they should not be included. Instead, I want to offer a space in this chapter to focus on content and the ways we can work with it. In many courses, the content is a given, understood to be correct. And while it might be challenging to learn, it is not (usually) challenged in terms of legitimacy. In our courses, however, this is not the case. We are challenged frequently about what we are presenting. In this way, our courses are part of a select group (e.g., evolution, climate change, women's studies) that deserve special consideration. I want to spend some time giving that consideration, focusing on what we can do with content and how we can do it in ways that might increase receptivity and understanding.

EXCEPTIONS, DISTRACTIONS, AND DISAGREEMENTS

If you teach college students, and particularly if your students are not wealthy enough to have their tuition and living expenses easily covered by family, then you are likely well aware of the financial pressures our students face. Students think about money and their lack of it a lot and it makes sense that their own needs will come up as they are learning more about racism and racial disparities. Consider the following scenario (some variation of which I have experienced many times): you are discussing the large wealth gaps between White and Black Americans. A White student objects, bringing up the fact that there are many relatively wealthy and prosperous Black Americans (e.g., LeBron James, Ben Carson). She goes on to say that her own White family is not wealthy and then compares herself to a wealthier Black person she knew in high school. That student, she says, received more scholarship money than she and other, poorer, White students did, so how is that fair?

There are many variations on this comment, and there is a lot that can be unpacked. In many ways, this comment exemplifies the differences between individual and institutional or aggregate thinking that I have described many times throughout this book. That is the fundamental gap in knowledge and understanding that I believe lies at the heart of understanding racism. Here, the student is pointing out an exception. A person who does not fit the story of the content and the evidence. In making this comment, the student seems to be resisting that larger story by focusing on a single, and highly personal, example. This can be frustrating, of course, but if you can keep that knowledge gap in mind and use it as a guide, it can help you navigate the comment in ways that reinforce the larger story of the content, while still maintaining trust.

First, there may be times when exceptions deserve recognition. As Kim Case points out in *Deconstructing Privilege*, "If students perceive an instructor as teaching dogma, they may resist learning new information" (p. 26, 2013). To keep our credibility, it can be useful not to contest single examples or specific instances, especially if those exceptions do not detract too much from the larger story of our content. For example, I have occasionally found myself in back-and-forth tug of wars with students over single facts. The student starts looking it up on their phone and I find myself wondering if it even really matters! At times, if we do not know the truth of a single fact or if that fact is not crucial, it is probably better to let it go and let the student keep the point they were making. Doing so helps us avoid the dogmatism that Case warns against and allows us to be flexible and honest, reinforcing our credibility. When we can let our students be right and follow new information (assuming it is credible), we model the very behavior we hope to instill.

The example of the "wealthy Black student," however, is not really that kind of exception. It is important to answer because it matters so much for understanding the larger truth of what racism is and how it operates in institutional and structural ways. In considering this particular comment, there are at least two problems. First, we do not know the wealth of any of these students. Second, and perhaps more importantly, it is well documented that there are large, persistent, and growing (at the time of this writing) gaps in wealth between White and Black Americans (Tatum, 2017). So how to proceed? First, allowing other students to comment before weighing in yourself can increase the likelihood that students will feel free to voice their opinions. If every problematic exception that is pointed out results in a quick and heavy-handed response from the instructor, disagreements may become private grudges. It is also likely that at least a few of the students will recognize the problem with the exception and point this out.

Next, remember that you can allow the exception while also modeling the use of scholarly evidence to try to answer the larger question. In this case, you might say that there are certainly people who are above or below the average when it comes to wealth for both Black and White Americans, but that this does not change the overall pattern of greater wealth for Whites. Men, on average, are taller than women are, but this does not mean that every man is taller than every woman is. Making this clear allows you to sidestep the anecdote, stay positive, and avoid directly challenging the student. I would urge this even as you might be tempted to ask just how it is that this student knows another family's bank balances or the Black student's aid situation. The problem with asking such questions is that there is no *evidence-based* way to find an answer and, even if there was, you are still focused just on that individual situation. Instead, go back to the use of evidence and to the larger story of the content. After pointing out that some folks are below or above the averages for the group, you can thank the student for the example and then turn the discussion toward the question underneath the student's question (and the one that they are likely asking): Is it really the case that Black students receive more college aid as compared to White students? Raising this particular question yourself and answering it with a scholarly article you can reference (Kantrowitz, 2011), discuss with students, and later post to the course learning management system can help to model the kind of evidence-based answer finding you hope to instill in your students. Better yet, it allows you to stay positive and connected to your student while being honest about racial disparities. Even if you do not know how to answer the deeper question involved, it is still worth pointing out that deeper question and then trying to find an evidence-based answer later that you can discuss or post. Again, it is important to get back to the larger story of the content and to do so in a way that models scholarly engagement and compassion.

Even when not pointing out exceptions, students can find other ways to derail our discussions. This happens, I think, because students are often so uncomfortable with the implications of the content and what it means for them personally. White students often feel guilty at the idea that they have received advantages because of their race while students of color often feel angry or disempowered by the vast nature of racism and its ability to limit their opportunities. Because feelings of guilt, anger, and hopelessness are so uncomfortable, students may try to distract away from the story of our content. Derald Wing Sue, in his 2015 book *Race Talk and the Conspiracy of Silence*, describes this phenomenon and argues that for those of us who facilitate discussions about race, an essential skill is the ability to control the process of discussion without worrying too much about the specifics of what participants say. He cites several examples of things that participants might proclaim (e.g., "racism happens in all countries, not just the United States"; "I experience sexism as a woman"), all of which are true on their face, but all of which distract away from the larger truth and story of our content. Sue recommends that when we get a distracting comment, we pause and ask the student how they are feeling and why they felt it important to make that particular comment (rather than addressing the substance of the comment). From there, you can ask other students if they have similar feelings and why they think these kinds of reactions are so common. Doing this accomplishes a few things. First, just as in the earlier example about financial aid, you are able to sidestep an unproductive argument over the truth of their statement. Second, you can help everyone to see or at least consider his or her own meta-affective reaction. Finally, you may help students see that they are not the only ones having difficult emotional reactions, thereby normalizing such feelings and increasing feelings of belonging.

THE IMPORTANCE OF INCLUSIVITY IN CONTENT

To begin this chapter, I described how White students often ask about the "other side." That is, when we will get to the part of the course that shows how White people are or have been the victims of racism. Similar questions come up around so-called reverse racism and the ways in which certain policies (especially affirmative action) might somehow benefit minorities above White people. When you understand how American racism works and how it developed, you know that you cannot answer those questions in a way that will feel satisfying to the White students who raise these objections. The truth is that beginning in the late 1600s, Whiteness was constructed specifically for the purpose of advantaging some people (those defined as White) so that they would not join forces with other people (those defined as Black and therefore enslaved) to rebel against rich landowners. This arrangement and the racist ideas it spawned to justify its existence have continued in various ways since that time (Kendi, 2016). Because of that legacy and the ways in which racism has been incorporated into our systems, policies, and beliefs, White people in the United States enjoy better outcomes as a group on every measure of life outcome. This is the structure of our society. There is a lot to understand about how and why this is so, but there is not a way to make it not true.

This reality is difficult enough for students to comprehend, but it is also amplified by the growing belief among many

White people in the United States that discrimination against Whites is increasing and that such discrimination is now as large or larger a problem than discrimination against racial minorities (Norton & Sommers, 2011; NPR, 2017). What this means is that we are often working against a perception of racism that is completely at odds with the reality of racism. To help our White students understand this reality, we have to find ways to include them in our curriculum. I admit that this does not feel fair, and I am certain that many people may disagree. It is tempting to ask, why do White people need to be included in everything? Especially when White people are the beneficiaries of racial privilege? The answer, I believe, lies in the importance of belonging for learning. To step back for a moment, consider that research has shown that White people do not associate "multiculturalism" or "diversity" with themselves (Plaut, Garnett, Buffardi, & Sanchez-Burks, 2011). Instead, initiatives around diversity or multiculturalism seem to make White people feel excluded, causing them to lower their support or engagement with such initiatives. Related research has shown that when companies and organizations take explicit steps to ensure that White people see themselves as part of multiculturalism and diversity, White participants increase their support, ultimately helping such initiatives to succeed (Stevens, Plaut, & Sanchez-Burks, 2008).

Translating this to the classroom, I believe that taking steps to make sure White students feel as if racism is important in their lives (and it is) may be essential to helping these students learn. To be clear, this does not mean that I endorse teaching false notions of White victimization or perpetuating the idea that White people lose just as much from the system of racism as people of color. That is not true. I also do not want to suggest that Whiteness should be at the center of everything in a course on race. Instead, I mean finding ways to talk about Whiteness as one part of the overall system of racism.

Whiteness and Blackness and the System of Racism

As noted throughout this book, understanding racism as a system (i.e., institutional) rather than as a personal character flaw (i.e., individual) is one of the key ways in which we as instructors often differ from most of our students. As Winkler (2018) described it, institutional racism is a "threshold concept," something that, once understood, helps students to understand everything else. One way to approach the concept of institutional racism is to start with its formation. Understanding that both Whiteness (those who were free) and Blackness (those who were enslaved) were creations of the early American elite and that these creations served a powerful economic motive (justifying slavery) allows for a clear and cohesive story of how we got our system of racism. Once that story is in place, other concepts make more sense as parts of the story. For example, race as a social construction. Students often have trouble with this idea; it can seem technical or abstract. But if you know that racial groups were created to justify particular economic motives, then this creation or "construction" is understandable. Similarly, an emphasis on both the creation of Whiteness and Blackness at a time when these were the only categories needed by the wealthy landowners (Native Americans had yet to be fully racialized, though this happened shortly) should help students to see that White is a race just as much any other.

Using the history of racial formation and including Whiteness and Blackness in that discussion as part of your content is what I mean by inclusivity. In this way, you include

White people as a race rather than as some unspoken norm, or worse as the "standard" racial group. In the story I describe above we are helping students see racial formation as an active process and Whiteness as a crucial part of that process. This may be very different from the version of racial history our students have received up to that point. As James Loewen pointed out in *Lies My Teacher Told Me* (2018), American history textbooks often describe Black enslavement and the theft of Native American land as passive occurrences, things that happened without real people driving the action. The more complete story I am suggesting includes both the enslaved and the enslavers. Moreover, it may help students better understand the complexities and nuances of the system. Wealthy White landowners were very different from poor, landless Whites, but Whiteness included them all and was a way for wealthy Whites to gain the support of poorer people.

Other Racial Groups Wedged Into the System

Depending on what you are teaching, it is likely that you will want to include racial groups beyond Black and White. Doing so is important not just because it is more inclusive, but because it allows students to better understand where we are now when it comes to racism in the United States. A broader focus will also speak more directly to students' everyday interracial experiences, especially if you live in a relatively diverse area or teach on a very diverse campus. Better understanding how all American racial groups have been formed and reformed, the unique issues groups face, and the ways in which different groups of color interact and perceive one another can add context across a variety of courses. Such context and knowledge should, in turn, help students consider their own interracial experiences through a larger and more contextualized framework of institutional racism.

To start, you may want to provide information about how other racial and ethnic groups have been created as part of the larger process of racial formation in the United States. Doing this allows you as an instructor to add to the existing story of Black-White racial formation (typically easier in terms of student learning and memory) rather than considering several separate stories. Even if you do not cover every group, you can still frame content about a specific group in terms of this larger story. Again, and from a broad perspective, as people have immigrated to the United States or had their lands taken or during times of war, all people in the United States have been racialized. Everyone has been made to fit somewhere along the continuum from Whiteness to Blackness. Some have been able to claim Whiteness (Painter, 2010), but others have been subsumed by large pan-ethnic labels such as Asian, Hispanic/Latino, or Middle Eastern. Some groups have also moved back and forth, gaining and losing Whiteness depending on the events of the time (Adelman, 2003). In building out the story, there are similarities across groups, but there are differences too. Presenting this kind of information can help instructors to include students from across the racial spectrum while also building student understanding of a broad and institutionalized system of race and racism that ensnares everyone.

One common theme across groups that you may want to emphasize is how racialization occurs as a way to justify economic exploitation. Marking a group of people as racialized and inferior helps to justify paying them low or no wages, stealing their land, or discarding and vilifying them during economic recessions. Whether it is Asian immigrants working on railroads or in sweatshops (Lee, 2015), the enslavement of Africans and Native Americans (Baptist, 2014; Reséndez, 2016), or the taking of land from Native people and Mexicans (Loewen, 2018), such exploitation has occurred across groups and in similar ways at different points in history. Seeing and understanding this helps students to better understand the roots of American racism and most students can then make connections between the history they are learning and the tensions and conflicts they see in their daily lives and in their news feeds.

Another useful theme within our history is how various groups have been pitted against each other in the service of rich and powerful White people. One important example of this is the way poor, landless Whites were deliberately racialized as White to prevent their making common cause with Blacks in early America (Isenberg, 2016). Along these same lines, most other racial groups, at different points in time, have been encouraged to avoid identifying too closely with Blacks. They have not been deemed White, but they have been encouraged to endorse White racist ideas as a way to become more accepted within American society. This rarely works (see the Cherokee people as just one example), but it often serves powerful White interests, reinforcing White supremacy and institutional racism and further enriching those powerful White interests (Adelman, 2003). As an instructor, you can choose which groups or examples you'd like to focus on, doing so as a way to help your students see similarities across history and across racial groups while also helping them make connections to the present day. Again, it might be useful to focus on the larger meta-story (keeping groups from uniting) as a way to contextualize and aid understanding of how individual racial and ethnic groups have come to where they are now.

Including White Privilege

In the last several years, the concept of White privilege and the notion of "checking your privilege" has gotten a lot of scrutiny on college campuses and in our divisive national discourse around identity, race, and politics. To see the range of reactions some people have to the notion of White privilege, try posting something on social media that references it. You will likely get some thoughtful responses, but you are also nearly guaranteed to experience some frustration. As an example, a friend of mine recently posted a comment on Facebook about a state legislator's complaints regarding our public university system. The legislator did not feel that students in our system should be learning about White privilege (he referenced a college course at the flagship University of Wisconsin in Madison). The reactions were swift and furious. Several of our mutual friends wrote that they agreed with the legislator, and that "human decency" was a more important lesson than White privilege. In addition, some argued that students could not learn about privilege from a class anyway, it had to be personal experience. In watching this response from seemingly liberal White people on Facebook, I was reminded of the central problem in all of our teaching about race and the one that I have been describing throughout this book: racism is more than just individual behaviors and feelings; it is a larger system within which we are all contained. Focusing on privilege, if not clearly defined, can take us back into the realm of individual behavior and feeling, reinforcing the gap of understanding that is present between our students and ourselves. It was obvious that those Facebook commenters, who so quickly moved to talk about their own experiences and the importance of "human decency" or "kindness," were not thinking about privilege as a systemic phenomenon advantaging their lives in myriad ways. Instead, they simply believed that so long as you are kind and nice to everyone, White privilege is irrelevant.

Despite these difficulties, those of us who teach about race know that teaching about White privilege is important. It is unavoidable for two reasons: 1) it is frequently front and center in national discussions around race, and 2) it is part of the institutional and structural nature of racism. Racism, because of how it works, advantages White Americans as a group. That advantage is privilege, and it is a necessary piece of understanding racism. So as an instructor, I include discussions of Whiteness and White privilege as a way to be inclusive, but also as a way to get at the differences between individual and systemic racism.

In teaching about White privilege, I try to choose content on White privilege that is less focused on individual experience as a way to get at the more systemic features. For example, many educators begin lessons on privilege with the classic Peggy McIntosh "knapsack" article (1988) in which the author lays out a listing of privileges that she herself experienced as a White woman. I understand this approach; I myself found this article extremely important as an undergraduate and graduate student. Nevertheless, this article and the use of it in teaching have been criticized for being too focused on individuals and for supporting the idea that privilege confession and individual behavioral change, rather than systemic change, are enough (Cabrera, 2017). Focusing just on getting students to confess or admit their privileges in ways similar to McIntosh can be counterproductive, provoking backlash and severing the connection students feel with us and with each other (Lensmire et al., 2013).

To get at the goal of systemic understanding, it might be helpful to combine provocative examples of individual privilege such as those found in that McIntosh article with a more comprehensive definition of privilege. For example, Eula Biss, in her 2015 essay "White Debt," describes privilege as a "legal system in which not everyone is equally bound." In other words, the laws do not apply in the same ways to everyone. Some are much more scrutinized than others. Similarly, Nolan L. Cabrera (2017) makes a convincing case for the idea of "white immunity" rather than White privilege. He writes, "it is not as much that Whites are raised (or privileged) by racism, but rather that People of Color are precluded from equitable treatment" (p. 82). These definitions may help students to see that privilege is not just about personal advantage (which many White students may not feel or see in their own lives), but about fair treatment. It is less about "me" as a person and more about a larger system that treats some groups more fairly than others and the unequal application of laws and policies across racial groups.

A big advantage of defining and thinking about privilege as immunity is how easily it maps onto examples that can then be more fully examined in class. One such example is the killing of unarmed Black men and women at the hands of police and other Americans. Since the 2012 killing of Trayvon Martin in Florida and especially after the protests that followed Michael Brown's killing and the lack of indictment for the White officer who shot him in 2014, extrajudicial shooting deaths of young Black men have received national attention and protest. Scholarly reports (Goff, Lloyd, Geller, Raphael, & Glaser, 2016), statistical analyses (Washington Post, 2017), and psychological studies (Mekawi & Bresin, 2015) bear out what we see in the press: those who are White experience the judicial system differently than those who are Black. White people experience less force at the hands of police, are less likely to be stopped, searched, or arrested, and are less likely to be shot as compared to Black people. Given the evidence, it is easy to see disparate treatment by race at the hands of a major American institution: the criminal justice system. Understanding this as immunity and as a difference in how laws are applied may help connect privilege back to the system of racism. To be clear, I have not yet seen this particular technique tested formally in the classroom. I have only just begun to teach privilege in this way, finding it useful for aiding understanding without eliciting as much resistance. In the future, it might be helpful to compare this approach to other approaches to better understand how learning about privilege works.

Another reason that focusing on privilege as immunity may be effective is that doing so can allow us to connect to intersectionality and to better understand how privilege and disadvantage work across identities. As I say frequently in class, all of us are a collection of social identities. Some of these identities advantage us while others disadvantage us, depending on the context and depending on how those identities interact. For example, as a woman, I am likely to experience sexism, but as a White woman, I also experience significant racial advantage. As noted back in Chapter 2, there is good reason to think that helping students to focus on both advantaged (privileged) and disadvantaged identities will lead to better understanding overall (Rosette & Tost, 2013; Wise & Case, 2013). Helping students to see the ways in which they may have been disadvantaged by identities such as social class, gender, religion, sexual orientation, and so on should be self-affirming. In turn, self-affirmation reduces threat, allowing students to be more open to learning about the privileges and advantages they hold.

Focusing on a broad array of identities also brings up new ways for students to see the larger systems at work. Consider the example of age. If your students are relatively young, they will no doubt have tales of adults who were suspicious of them or did not trust them based on their age. We have policies and norms that codify these suspicions, extending benefits to people based on age that are not given to those considered too young (voting, consumer purchases, differential applications of the law). As we age, we may experience new and different protections as well as new and different disadvantages. Sexual orientation, gender, and education level also provide a host of examples and help students to see the ways in which we protect some groups of people over others in formal and informal ways. To return to my earlier example of extrajudicial killings, the same statistics showing disparate treatment by race also show disparate treatment with respect to those who are mentally ill (those with mental illness are overrepresented in the killings) and with respect to age (those who are under 30 are overrepresented in the killings). This technique is not meant to detract from the primacy of race in our discussions, but instead to offer students a variety of ways to connect with the concept of racial privilege.

Finally, it can be useful to talk about White privilege in terms of both benefits and costs. Professor David Shih, a colleague of mine from the University of Wisconsin–Eau Claire, has a couple of blog posts that describe these costs ("White Supremacy Can Make You Poor," 2015; "White Happened to You," 2015), and the activist Tim Wise discusses these costs in his book *White Like Me* (2011). Discussing how White supremacy and racism isolate us from each other and cost us financially may be a great way to help students think more complexly about privilege and about racism as a system. For example, I have found that White students often worry that others will see them as racist just because they are White.

These fears are very real and important for many of them (they are traditional age college students) and discussing that fear as part of the larger system of racism and stereotypes may be a good way to help them see the interpersonal consequences of racism. As with the idea of defining privilege as immunity, I have not yet seen research on this technique in the classroom, but my own experience with students has been very positive so far. There are lots of interesting costs to consider, some at the system level (financial and material costs) and others at the personal level (stereotypes, fears), and a lot of ways that this can complicate and nuance your discussions of racism and racial privilege with students.

CONTENT DELIVERY

If you strip down the job of an instructor, what does it consist of? I would argue that one of our most basic functions, particularly in this time of easy access to heaps and heaps of information, is providing students with information they can trust and then setting up activities and assessments that will help students transform that information into knowledge. Obviously, we want to do more than deliver content, and many of our objectives are focused on skills development as much as knowledge acquisition, but it can be helpful to begin with this simplified formula: good information accompanied by activities that help students transform that information into knowledge and understanding. Along the way, we can focus in on particular skills and their development, but we often start with content. In this section, I will focus on content delivery and the evidence that supports particular ways of doing that. Ways that decrease resistance and help students grapple with the overwhelming realities of racism.

The Importance of Narrative and Story

A few years ago, I was reading the excellent 2014 book *The Half Has Never Been Told: Slavery and the Making of American Capitalism* by historian Edward Baptist. I recommended this book earlier, and I think it is an excellent way to learn more about how slavery was experienced by those who were enslaved and how slavery evolved to fit the economic desires of the enslavers and of the American economy more broadly. I learned many things in reading this book, but what I remember first when I think back on it are the stories that Baptist used to begin each chapter or illustrate particular points. For example, the story of a young Black woman arriving in New Orleans in 1819, a woman he called "Rachel." Baptist described what she would have seen as she arrived, where she would have been taken, and how she would have been sold. In reading about Rachel, I was learning about the importance of New Orleans in the slave trade and why it became such an important hub as slavery became more profitable, expanding westward with slave labor camps along the Mississippi River. There are many other stories like this in the book, and all of them helped me to imagine the historical facts described in the text and to remember them after I had finished reading. This is not just my experience; many of us know this feeling well and there is good evidence that stories are particularly helpful for learning and memory. For our purposes, stories and narrative may be especially useful in teaching about race.

For a 2009 study, Nancy Chick, Terri Karis, and I asked students in four different race-related courses (including psychology, literature, and geography) what helped them learn. We asked them to report this out at several points during the semester. One clear finding from our surveys was the importance of narrative and story. Students in each course focused in on particular pieces of content (assigned readings, video, audio) and even specific examples from within those pieces that were stories. For example, the narratives of enslaved people assigned by Nancy in her African American literature course. For that course, students noted that reading such stories helped them to empathize with the plight of enslaved people and to realize that many Americans at the time did not consider slaves human. Across all of the courses we studied, students mentioned the importance of narrative and story repeatedly, noting particular examples that were helpful and describing how much they felt they had learned from reading these stories.

One reason for this may be that stories simply require less cognitive space, making learning easier. Working memory is limited. We cannot hold that much information in our minds at any one time. But as Sarah Cavanagh describes in her 2016 book *The Spark of Learning*, stories work as "holistic narrative[s] tied together by meaning" (p. 89). In other words, stories link information together through meaning, ultimately taking less space and attention. As a result, we can remember stories more easily as compared to a bunch of isolated facts or ideas. Thinking back to the story of Rachel disembarking from the ship in New Orleans in Edward Baptist's book, I can remember that her journey represents a significant shift in how slavery worked. Recalling this, I can then more easily remember some of the reasons for that shift: the planting of cotton and its use in northern and British factories, the changes to banking in the United States, and the consequences of that shift for the people who were enslaved. That story connects, through meaning and narrative, to a bunch of other facts that I might not remember as easily if they were only abstract and discrete pieces of information.

In addition to remembering the content, stories may also increase our ability to empathize with characters and situations we might not otherwise encounter, thus increasing our understanding and learning. In a review of the literature published in 2014, Djikic and Oatley described a variety of studies showing how reading literature, especially literary fiction, can increase our ability to empathize and to understand the emotion of others. That same review showed that reading fiction could decrease prejudice as readers take on the perspective of a fictional character who is different from themselves in terms of race and/or religion.

Scientists are still sorting out why this happens, but there are interesting clues to suggest that a part of the reason for this involves the ways in which fiction transports us into the lives of others and allows us to open our minds to their experience. When we read a story, we can "*think along* and even *feel along*" with the character (Djikic, Oatley, & Moldoveanu, 2013, p. 150, emphasis in the original). That is, we are encouraged to simulate the feelings and experiences of other people rather than focusing on ourselves. Moreover, this happens even when we dislike the character! In another interesting finding, Djikic and colleagues showed that those who read short fictional stories (as compared to those who read nonfiction essays) showed a decrease in the need for cognitive closure and a decrease in discomfort with ambiguity. In other words, reading allows us to suspend our need to make judgments, helping us to think about others in a broader and more empathic way, even as those characters are doing things or experiencing things very different from us. As the authors put it, "When reading about fictional characters, one does not feel the need to defend one's perspective. One can simulate the workings of other minds without the fear of undermining one's own" (p. 153).

Taken together, these findings present a strong case for using narrative in our content whenever possible. The scientific work to date suggests that literary fiction and short stories might work best, but research has not yet fully examined all types of narrative, especially in the classroom. My own suggestion would be to use narrative in a variety of formats (fiction, video clips, film, memoir, journalistic accounts, etc.) and to combine such content with the broader, more abstract information you are trying to cover (statistics, policies, theories, findings, etc.). To take just one example, I cover interracial dating and marriage toward the end of my course, and I like to spend some time helping students think about how racism informs our notions of what is beautiful and attractive. To do this, I have recently used an essay written by Noah Cho (2014) about his struggles with body image as an Asian American man. In it, he describes his desire to look Whiter. He also describes the stereotypes that inform our thinking about Asian men (i.e., meekness, femininity) and about how these stereotypes have affected his thinking about himself. To supplement this first-person account, I also provide statistics about dating and marriage that show how race and gender affect desirability in the dating market. Not surprisingly, Asian men tend to fare worse (as do Black women). This approach, combining narrative with broader statistics, not only generates useful discussion (Cho's essay in particular), but it also provides a way to connect broader stereotypes and inequalities to the story of an individual person. In seeing the perspective of Cho, the students can begin to understand why the statistics matter.

The Importance of Active Engagement

It is a truism in the scholarship of teaching and learning that active learning is effective. Regardless of format (lecture, discussion, online, face-to-face), it is important to get students involved and engaged with the content as opposed to passive listening. When it comes to learning about race, this is no less true. Corrine Moss-Racusin and her colleagues, in their review of scientific diversity interventions (Moss-Racusin et al., 2014), list "active learning techniques" as one of the four essential design elements for successful diversity education and bias reduction (the others are rigorous evaluation, avoiding blame, and grounding your techniques in evidence). Actively engaging with the content can take many forms: engaging mini-lectures interspersed with writing or discussion activities, in-class games, small groups work, and so on. For now, I will focus in on discussion, largely because I believe it provides unique benefits within a course on race.

As I have noted at several points already, there are many good reasons to get students talking. Discussion can increase feelings of belonging, which, in turn, increases course enjoyment and may even improve grades. Discussion also helps students to see that their reactions to the content are normal, that they are not (in general) any less informed, having a more difficult time understanding, or having a more emotional response (guilt, anger, etc.) than their peers. When it comes to race, a subject so many people struggle to contend with, it is even more key to make student reactions to content visible in the ways that discussion can make possible.

But if you have taught with discussion you know that discussion does not usually "just happen." It is not enough to give students interesting content, ask them to read, and expect them to be come to class ready to chat. Simply asking students to read and discuss will often result in very quiet classrooms. The main reason for this silence, according to Jay Howard, the author of the 2015 book *Discussion in the*

College Classroom, is lack of confidence. As Howard details, research has shown that students often do not feel confident that what they have to say is important enough or accurate enough to break through the strong norms for nonparticipation present in most college classrooms.

To get past this silence and to be intentional in our efforts to get students discussing the content, there are a lot of evidence-based techniques for bypassing the lack of confidence and the norms that pressure students into silence (see Howard's book for a great review). One over-arching feature of many of these techniques involves designing your courses so that reading and discussion are explicitly incentivized. Assigning the content is not enough. To get active engagement, we have to make engagement with content part of the structure of points and rewards. As one example, I ask my students to read course content ahead of time, posting their responses to the online course management system. Once posted, I grade the responses according to a rubric and then use those responses (or a random sampling) to help facilitate in-class discussions. This happens on most days of the course for me, but you could certainly vary how much you use it, saving it for particular assignments or sections of the course. The important point is to make discussion an incentivized and regular feature of your class time. It can be useful to remember that you can add incentives for both the reading and preparation part (content quizzes, posted responses) as well as for the in-class participation part (attendance, participation points). Whatever you do, do not leave discussion to chance. If you want to teach with discussion, it is important to be intentional about how students will receive credit for their efforts.

Another important factor to consider when designing discussions is structure. As noted above, confidence is a major barrier to student participation (Howard, 2015). Many students simply will not speak up unless they are sure they are right. My own daughter, home for her first Thanksgiving break after beginning college, explained that she never spoke in class to answer the professor's questions unless she was absolutely sure she had the "right answer." Even then, she was really only speaking up to spare the professor's feelings. She just could not see discussion as valuable at all and in that context, it probably was not. Simply throwing out questions that seem to have "right" and "wrong" answers is probably not a useful way to get students thinking about and engaged with the content. Instead, most students in that context are worrying more about how they will look or sound to their classmates. To get beyond these concerns, research suggests that structured experiences are more effective (Parrott & Cherry, 2011). Giving explicit instructions or steps for students to follow, assigning students specific tasks or roles, allowing them time to think or write about their responses prior to talking, and "ramping up" to whole-class discussions with small groups discussions are all ways to lower the stakes and clarify the rules for engagement so that students feel more confidence in their ability to participate (Howard, 2015).

SUMMARIZED RECOMMENDATIONS AND SUGGESTIONS

Sidestep Distractions and Exceptions

As important as it is to get students talking about the content, there are definitely times when their comments and questions are a challenge to one's commitment to active learning. Fortunately, there are ways to work with such comments and questions to reinforce the larger story of the content while still maintaining student trust and increasing learning. To do so, I think it is helpful to think in terms of a few guiding questions.

First, is the comment really just an exception or an anomaly that is not worth fully considering? There may be times when students raise objections or exceptions to the content you are providing that are truly exceptions or that are not truly answerable in any meaningful way. These kinds of questions are not really worth the time it would take to unpack them and are really just distractions away from the larger message. The most common examples of these usually involve individual people of color who are incredibly successful or individual White people who are not (the former usually celebrities or Barack Obama, the latter usually people they know or know of). When such exceptions are raised, it can be helpful to acknowledge that these exceptions do not fit the larger patterns of privilege and discrimination and move on. One trap that is easy to fall into is trying to find out more information about the exception so as to prove the larger point. For example, asking questions about the White person they know (the one who has no advantage) so as to find out more and, perhaps, be able to show some hidden privileges. The problem here is that there is no real, objective way to find out more information about the exception and so such exercises are usually unconvincing to the student who raised the objection and a little boring for everyone else in the class. Better to let the exception go and move on to other comments and ideas. Doing so reinforces student trust in you (you are not being dogmatic or defensive) and keeps you on track.

A second question to ask as you work with difficult comments: what is the larger question or issue at play here? Earlier I gave the example of a White student asking about a Black student she had known who, despite being apparently wealthy, had received considerable college aid. In this situation, the real question seems to be: why do students of color get more financial aid than White students? Focusing on this question and using evidence to answer it (they do not actually receive more aid), either in the moment or later after you or the students themselves have had time to gather the evidence, is a much more powerful way to reinforce the larger story of the content you are teaching.

In addition to questions that are really questions about something else, there may also be times when the real issue is about student emotion and feeling. Anger, guilt, hopelessness, and so on can often be expressed through distracting comments and questions about unrelated ideas. Here again, it is probably helpful to try and get at the underlying emotion rather than trying to answer each question perfectly or taking them all at face value. Perhaps it would help to ask the students to write reflectively for a few minutes about how they are feeling or to break into smaller groups' discussion (this also might allow you to talk to the student more directly). Overall, when working with exceptions and distractions, the idea is to try and move back toward the larger story of the content, using evidence and staying focused on the overarching point or message.

Include Racialized Groups, Even White People

The importance of including all racialized groups in your content is not to suggest some sort of false equivalence, but rather to ensure that all racialized groups, including White people, are understood to be races. Whites are a privileged and advantaged race to be sure, but a race nonetheless. To be inclusive, it can be helpful to focus in on the process of racial formation. Luckily there are a lot of great resources available to help with this. In addition to short chapters or readings from authors like Audrey Smedley (2007) or Michael Omi and Howard Winant (2015), I might especially recommend a recent podcast series from the show *Scene on Radio*. This series, called *Seeing White* and produced by the Center for Documentary Studies at Duke University, does a really nice job of explaining the basics of racial formation to a general audience. The host interviews a variety of historians and several individual episodes from the series could provide a great starting point for discussion, particularly Parts 2, 3, and 4 (Biewen, 2017). The Appendix also provides several suggestions that are relatively accessible and can help you and your students better understand our racial history and the themes I described earlier. Many of these sources focus in on specific groups of people and how they became racialized in the course of American history.

In addition to providing historical content, you may also want to discuss and describe how different racial groups perceive one another and the unique issues that each racial group faces in American society. Pew Research regularly conducts attitude surveys across a variety of racial groups. Other organizations have done so as well (NPR, Public Religion Research Institute), providing current data that students can read and discuss in light of their own feelings and experiences. Depending on your campus, you may also be able to access campus climate data that breaks out the experiences of students by race, gender, and other factors. Examining the attitudes and experiences of other students on your own campus can be especially engaging and can help to put larger trends into perspective. You could also use novels, short stories, plays, or other forms of art to help students take on the perspectives of various racial groups. Finally, I would strongly recommend Beverly Daniel Tatum's updated classic *Why Are All the Black Kids Sitting Together in the Cafeteria?* In it, she has an entire section devoted to the critical issues of identity development common to people from each of a variety of racial groups (Latinx, Native American, Middle Eastern/North African, Asian and Pacific Islander), including those who are multiracial. These chapters are very well researched and thorough and may help to provide you with the background information you need to have productive classroom discussions.

If White privilege is a part of your course content, and I would argue it really should be if you are discussing White people as a racialized group, it can be helpful to focus on privilege and advantage in a few specific ways. Most importantly, White privilege is pervasive, expressing itself in daily life as an ongoing immunity to the problems and struggles that other racialized people have to deal with. Seeing that immunity, that privilege, can be difficult for students. Privilege is so often invisible to those experiencing it. One way to make this easier is to help students think across their identities using an exercise created by Margalynne J. Armstrong and Stephanie M. Wildman. Writing in a 2013 chapter from the book *Deconstructing Privilege,* they describe the "Power Line Exercise." This activity asks students to identify different pieces of their social identities (e.g., race, class, religion, gender, ability) as "above or below" the line with respect to social privilege. After spending some time working alone, the students share (via small groups first and then as part of the whole class) how they decided if their identity pieces were above or below the line and how they felt about the activity. I use a variation of this myself, described earlier in Chapter 2, as a way to decrease resistance. I like doing it because research has shown that claiming a less privileged identity is a good way to help people more easily accept and understand their privileged selves (Rosette & Tost, 2013; Wise & Case, 2013). In addition, I have found that talking across identity pieces in this way allows for a better discussion of the institutional and structural forces that underpin advantage and disadvantage in daily life.

Deliver the Content in Ways That Increase Engagement

As Ken Bain describes in his wonderful 2004 book *What the Best College Teachers Do,* the best teachers are those who invite students into their discipline as if inviting them to a "feast." This invitation, he argues, can provide students with a sense of control over their own learning even as the instructor retains the power to "set the table." As you set that table, it can be helpful to be transparent and open about how you came to use the information that is included. For example, early in a semester, I often do a short presentation about how a few particular pieces (things assigned to them for class) made the cut. If it is a scientific article, I talk about the other work that supports it and the place it holds in the larger scientific literature. If it is a more general audience piece (news, commentary, etc.), I discuss why I use such pieces alongside scholarly and original sources, acknowledging that I do this in part because these pieces are usually shorter and easier to read. I then ask students (working in small groups) to identify a few of the main arguments in one of the news pieces. Finally, I show them the evidence (the scholarly sources) that support the arguments they have uncovered. My goal is to make my vetting process and the disciplinary standards that I use clearer to them. I have not formally tested this particular technique to see if it increases trust in the content or engagement in class, but I have noticed that students will often ask me about things they have seen themselves, both as we are doing the activity and especially in emails after class. Often, they want to mimic my vetting process, but need help determining the reliability of their sources. I encourage this and have often responded to emails from students months or even years after they have taken the course.

In addition to being transparent, you can increase engagement through the use of narrative and story in your content. As noted earlier, stories not only make comprehension and remembering easier, but they also seem to allow us to empathize with people and situations that may be very different from ourselves. As a result, stories and narratives across racial groups can help students see how the evidence they are learning about is embodied and experienced. Short stories, memoir, documentaries, and news stories can all provide powerful narrative examples of the content you are trying to cover. One technique I use a lot is to pair statistical evidence of racial disparities with stories about the people who are experiencing those disparities. For example, there are large and well-documented differences between White people and people of color when it comes to health. Within those health disparities, we know that Black people have much higher maternal death rates and infant mortality rates as compared to others. Sharing those numbers along with compelling interviews or news stories about the women (including famous women like Serena Williams) who have encountered serious complications, died, or coped with infant mortality can help students make sense of the ways in which these disparities affect real people. Finding good stories about race and racism is usually just a matter of paying closer attention to quality news sources, especially longer magazine-like pieces, podcasts, and some short blog posts. My current favorites are NPR (especially the *Code Switch* blog and podcast) and *This American Life*. Both have made efforts to diversify their contributors in recent years and it shows in the kinds of stories being produced and the perspectives they are told from.

Finally, there are lots of examples of in-class activities and discussion prompts in the literature that you can use to try and increase engagement. *Teaching for Diversity and Social Justice* (Adams et al., 2016) provides a broad overview and a lot of ideas, but you can also find discipline-specific ideas within the teaching literature of your own field, and I would suggest doing a quick search of the major teaching journal for your field if you have not already done so. Using evidence-based strategies that provide students with structured opportunities to think about, reflect on, and discuss their ideas often works well. One recent example that stands out to me comes from Winkler (2018) as part of her African American studies course. Specifically, she asked students to define the word "racism" at several points throughout the semester. The students first did this individually, as part of an in-class writing activity, eventually moving into small groups discussion and finally into whole-class discussion. You may recall that Winkler was interested in how students begin to understand racism as institutional rather than just individual. Along the way, they had lectures and readings to complete, but they kept returning to this in-class activity of writing, discussing, and reporting out. She did this both as a way to assess their learning but also as a catalyst for their learning. In this way, she was able to use one of her most central learning objectives (seeing racism as more than just individual) and make it into a structured and recurring class activity.

CONCLUSION AND
SUMMARY OF IDEAS

—

THE LAST FEW YEARS have seen an increase in the number of publicized incidents on college campuses involving professors and students and conflicts about race. In some instances, instructors have lost their positions or been placed on leave, with this happening most often to those who are the least powerful: contingent or adjunct faculty and faculty of color. In other situations, instructors keep their positions but experience harassment and threats, particularly online. Again, this has happened most often to instructors of color. Each case has its own unique circumstances and nuances, of course, and many of the most high-profile cases have not even involved the classroom. In many of those cases, an instructor's Twitter comments involving race and injustice are then amplified by right-wing media outlets, bouncing across the blogosphere and mainstream media. Typically, the comments are out of context or misunderstood (recall Saida Grundy and the ways in which her language as a sociologist was misconstrued).

In writing this book, I have not focused on that kind of race talk. Instead, I have tried to focus in on the classroom.

Unlike social media, the classroom offers a bit more control and a chance to slow things down. With the help of the research and ideas I have provided, I hope that you can use that classroom, your classroom, to teach in ways that are both compassionate and ruthlessly honest. I believe that most of us who teach about race want the same thing: students who have accurate knowledge, an ability to be critical about what they are hearing about race, and the skills and self-confidence necessary to join the larger, faster, and more fraught conversations happening outside our classrooms. I hope that I have given you some ways to move closer to this with your own students.

To wrap up, I want to list a few of the overarching ideas that I believe cut across the content of this book. These are the ideas that inspired me to write, the ones that I find myself returning to again and again.

1. *Experts on race and racism understand race differently than most Americans (including students).* In the powerful video series *Race: The Power of an Illusion* (Adelman, 2003), the narrator asserts that in the early to mid-nineteenth century, just as the country was being torn apart by questions of Native American removal and slavery, the majority of Whites in the general public held an understanding of race that was not that different than the experts of the time. Back then, so-called scientific books on race (e.g., *Types of Mankind*, Nott & Gliddon, 1854) sold out quickly, and ideas that would now be called scientific racism were considered legitimate. These days, experts and the public are further apart. As documented back in Chapter 1, most Americans espouse notions of colorblindness and think about racism as something that is primarily individual, not institutional or structural. This gap makes our job as instructors more difficult, but it gives

us an important learning objective for our courses: bridging that gap and helping our students see racism for what it is, institutional and structural in addition to personal.

2. *Resistance is normal and (somewhat) predictable.* As outlined back in Chapter 2, there are many psychological reasons for student resistance, and these reasons help us understand why students resist. Resistance can also take many forms: cognitive (rationalization and justifications), affective (anger, hopelessness), and behavioral (disengagement, protest). In recognizing resistance, we see that learning is not really a linear process. Instead, students circle back repeatedly to earlier understandings. This is frustrating, of course, but knowing why and how it happens can help us better understand the learning process and prepare for it more effectively. We can also be more aware of how resistance and classroom experience differ because of the racial identity and experience of each of our students.

3. *Acceptance and affirmation are useful tools for learning.* There are a lot of difficult things to accept about our students and about the learning process (e.g., that many will see things differently than we do, that they will resist, that they will learn in nonlinear ways). The good news, though, is that through accepting our students and affirming them whenever possible, we are likely to decrease resistance and increase student learning. It may feel counterintuitive, but most of the evidence from the psychological and teaching literatures suggests that affirming our students rather than confronting them will be more effective. As noted in the chapter on resistance, we may get more understanding if we first (or simultaneously) allow privileged students to affirm their own less advantaged identities. This may feel unfair or as though we are somehow letting White students "off the hook," but if the ultimate goal is the understanding of

privilege, it makes sense to use the most effective means available. Affirmation is also important for students of color. Affirming these students' experiences with racism and letting them know that they only have to represent themselves can help to increase trust and decrease withdrawal.

Repeatedly, and across chapters, I have tried to show how affirmation and acceptance of our students as they are, rather than as we wish them to be, can increase learning. Letting go of compelling our students or trying to make them be exactly what we want them to be is ultimately much more effective. When students feel accepted, they experience less threat and greater autonomy, helping them open to new ideas and resist defensiveness. This can be hard for us as instructors, particularly when the stakes feel so high and we really want them to understand how important the problems of racism and White supremacy are. But, letting go of some of our control and placing our trust in the process will ultimately lead to more learning.

4. *Belonging and connection are powerful.* The most powerful idea I want to share is that belonging really matters. Belonging is a fundamental human motive. We all want to feel a part of the group, to feel that we are accepted, and that others understand us. As instructors, we can leverage these powerful feelings and try to create classrooms that are warm and positive and that help students feel connected to us and to each other. Doing this, research suggests, helps students enjoy our courses more and learn better, even when that learning is difficult and disruptive to their sense of themselves and of the world.

Creating a warm and inclusive classroom is not easy. As noted in Chapter 3, instructors face a lot of difficulty in teaching about race. We have to juggle our own feelings while also attending to the feelings of our students. We also need to be sensitive to the external pressures we face and to the job security threats that can arise when we receive lower teaching evaluations. These threats are especially likely for instructors marginalized by race, lack of tenure, and/or adjunct status. There are things we can do for ourselves to try to mitigate these difficulties, but we also need the support of administration and of our fellow instructors. Having such support is critical to the learning of our students. As we feel supported, we can then support our students and help them to feel included.

5. *Shame and blame are powerful too.* The other side of connection and belonging is shame and blame. Fundamentally, shame and blame are about being "bad" people. That is, we believe (or feel others believe) that we have done something that makes us irredeemable. When we feel this way, our defenses naturally come up and learning becomes elusive. As you know from your own experience and as outlined throughout this book, learning about race is often very threatening to the self, a threat that takes on different dimensions depending on the student. Pervasive racial discrimination can threaten White students' sense that their own achievement is legitimate while students of color may doubt whether they can achieve at all.

   For all students, doubling down on this threat through harsh or confrontational lessons is ineffective. Instead, it pays to be sensitive to these threats. To work to lessen their impact. This means creating classrooms that are compassionate and forgiving, allowing for growth and change, expecting and rewarding active engagement, and empowering our students through our assignments and our activities. In short, we have to help them move away from simply blaming themselves or feeling ashamed of how racism has or might affect them. That is often a dead end of bad feelings and inaction. Instead, I believe that we can help students take responsibility for their own role in racism by showing them the true scale of how racism works (institutional and structural) and helping them see that learning about racism and understanding their own connection to it is rewarding and important.

6. *Perfection is unlikely.* Learning is a messy and an imperfect process characterized by moves forward and steps back. That said, students can learn, and we can teach in ways that help to ensure that learning. Holding an expectation of growth for ourselves and being explicit about it with our students can lead to a host of positive outcomes. Research shows that growth mindsets are beneficial for learning and that they allow us to take responsibility for and learn from our mistakes. Research in the classroom, in particular, has shown that inducing a growth mindset via our comments and feedback can increase student use of that feedback and reduce the risk that students will cheat. Given the sensitive nature of race and the fear that people have about saying the "wrong thing," messages about the possibility of growth and change and the acceptance of mistakes as part of that process may be an especially welcome relief. Here again, we see the paradoxical nature of teaching and learning about race: when we let go of tough, controlling tactics and allow space for both mistakes and the messy process of learning, we can help our students get closer to the outcomes we most want.

7. *Race is about everyone.* Often courses about race are seen as primarily about people of color. But the truth is that racism is about everyone. Broadly speaking, the problems caused by racism stem from the racist ideas developed primarily by White people. Those who are or have been designated "non-White" are then subject to these racist ideas and suffer as a result. Being racialized and socialized into this system of

racist ideas is a process that all Americans experience and for which all Americans pay a price. The costs are much less steep for Whites of course, but the costs are real even as they are harder to see.

Including as many racialized groups as possible into the content of your course is a powerful way to help students understand how race and racism work. There are many ways to do this, including the use of historical information about racial formation for different groups, literature from across groups, sociological and other statistics showing disparities, and psychological findings documenting the effects of racism. However you do it, the idea is to be inclusive and help students see how racism works as a larger system that affects everyone in ways both similar and profoundly different. Research suggests that including everyone is both engaging and empowering, likely because it allows students to find their place and make what they are learning more meaningful to themselves. If we want our students to feel empowered and educated enough to take anti-racist action, they have to find their entry point.

Appendix

—

SUGGESTED READING FOR HISTORICAL UNDERSTANDING

—

THIS LIST is by no means complete, but simply represents some of the works that have been the most helpful to me as I have worked to understand American history with the goal of providing important context for my students around racial history. I do not assign these works (though I have sometimes assigned excerpts); instead I reference them during class discussion and provide them in a course resource list along with several other kinds of resources (podcasts, people to follow on Twitter, etc.). Again, this list is not meant to be exhaustive but is meant to provide ideas for further reading.

Adelman, L. (Producer). (2003). *Race: The power of an illusion.* [Television Series]. San Francisco, CA: California Newsreel.

This three-part, nonfiction series covers several important issues with respect to race and racism, using a variety of experts from across a wide spectrum of disciplines. Volume one focuses on what race is and the myth of its biological essentialism. Some parts of this volume may feel a little dated (genes and genetics), but overall the science presented is accurate and can easily be supplemented with additional discussion and/or readings. Volumes two and three are especially helpful in understanding American racial history and the racialization of White Americans, Black Americans, Native Americans, Middle Eastern Americans, Asian Americans, and Mexican Americans. The focus on important court cases that helped to define Whiteness along with the roles played by science and government policy in reinforcing White supremacy is very helpful to student understanding of racism as an enduring institution.

Anderson, C. (2016). *White rage: The unspoken truth of our racial divide.* New York, NY: Bloomsbury.

This nonfiction book was written by Emory University historian Carol Anderson. A relatively short book, this work focuses on particular moments in American history and how White Americans at each point have engaged in acts of oppression and violence in response to Black American progress. These moments include the deconstruction of reconstruction, the response to *Brown v. Board*, and the election of President Obama, among others. Throughout, the author shows how laws, policies, and acts of violence have been used to stop racial progress and to maintain racial hierarchy.

Baptist, E. E. (2014). *The half has never been told: Slavery and the making of American capitalism.* New York, NY: Basic Books.

This nonfiction book was written by Cornell University historian Edward Baptist. In it, the author traces the development of slavery across time in the United States, outlining how slavery contributed to the economic development of the country. He busts several myths about slavery along the way, most notably debunking the idea that slavery would have naturally disappeared over time without the Civil War. Instead, he documents how valuable slaves as property truly were and how enslavers worked to ensure their own continued profit. Finally, Baptist helps the reader understand how slavery felt to those who were enslaved and how the system affected all facets of American life, then and now.

Blackmon, D. A. (2008). *Slavery by another name: The re-enslavement of Black Americans from the Civil War to World War II*. New York, NY: Doubleday.

A nonfiction book of history written by an award-winning journalist and author, Douglas Blackmon. Blackmon writes about how slavery evolved, after the Civil War, into a new form of neo-slavery. As he lays out, laws across the country, but concentrated in the South, effectively criminalized much of Black life. Caught up in this cycle, men (almost exclusively Black) were sold to work in dangerous and deadly forced labor camps as a way to repay their criminal debts. These debts were rarely paid (the terms often changed as time went on) and many languished in these prison camps for years. Death and disease were rampant. Blackmon shows how state and local governments were complicit in this scheme, how the federal government refused to help these enslaved Americans, and how businesses and corporations both large and small benefitted materially.

Isenberg, N. (2016). *White trash: The 400-year untold history of class in America*. New York, NY: Viking.

This nonfiction book was written by Louisiana State University historian Nancy Isenberg. Beginning with the Puritans and moving through to the present day, the author shows how poor Whites have been used to ensure political gains for White people in the middle and upper classes. Isenberg clearly shows how social mobility has been promised and how it has been taken away through a survey of political rhetoric, social policy, and popular culture across 400 years of American history. This book also helps the reader better understand how class and race are inextricably linked and how poor White Americans and their categorization by social class helps to reinforce racial categorization and hierarchy.

Kendi, I. (2016). *Stamped from the beginning: The definitive history of racist ideas in America.* New York, NY: Nation Books.

This nonfiction book was written by American University historian Ibram Kendi. A winner of the National Book Award, this book covers the history of anti-Black racist ideas in the United States from its founding through the election of President Obama. Over and over, Kendi persuasively shows how racist ideas have served the political and material interests of the elite while damaging other Americans, especially Black people and poor Whites. Kendi provides the most clear and convincing explanation of what racism is and how it operates that I have ever read.

Lee, E. (2015). *The making of Asian America: A history.* New York, NY: Simon and Schuster.

A nonfiction book of history written by University of Minnesota historian Erika Lee. This exhaustive book traces the lives and experiences of those we now call Asian Americans from their first arrival in the Americas through to the present day. Examining each national group in turn, Lee examines how laws and policies, the persecution by other Americans, and the exploitation of labor contributed to the experiences and identities of Asian Americans in the United States and, to a lesser extent, Canada. She highlights and deeply examines some events especially closely, including the detention of Japanese Americans and the experiences of the Hmong during and after the Vietnam War.

Loewen, J. W. (1995; 2018). *Lies my teacher told me: Everything your American history textbook got wrong.* New York, NY: Touchstone.

A winner of the American Book Award in 1996, this nonfiction book written by sociologist James Loewen describes how American history, as taught in American schools, has been biased in favor of White Americans and has perpetuated a number of falsehoods. The chapters cover a broad range of topics, but several chapters focus on race with respect to the teaching of slavery, the lack of teaching around anti-racism in American history, and the teaching of Native American genocide. An updated edition with a new preface focused on the election of Donald Trump was published in 2018.

Painter, N. I. (2010). *The history of White people.* New York, NY: W.W. Norton and Company.

A nonfiction book of history written by Princeton historian Nell Irvin Painter. This exhaustive book traces the development of the idea of Whiteness, beginning with the ancient Greeks, but focused most intensely on how Americans have defined White-ness. Painter describes and explains how Whiteness has been "enlarged" to include different groups of Americans at different points in our history and for different political and economic reasons. This book does an excellent job of showing how powerful people wield their power to shape identity in ways that help them to retain their power and keep out groups of people they deem un-American.

Reséndez, A. (2016). *The other slavery: The uncovered story of Indian enslavement in America.* New York, NY: Houghton Mifflin.

A nonfiction book of history written by University of California–Davis historian Andres Reséndez, this book uncovers and details the ways in which Caribbean and American Indians were systematically enslaved by the Spanish from 1492 through 1900. Describing it as the "other" slavery to distinguish it from the African slave trade, the author provides important details about how the enslavement of Indians morphed and changed over time in response to economic and political pressures and how it was both similar to and different from the African slave trade. The author focuses particularly on the American Southwest and how this other slavery coexisted with African slavery through the American Civil War.

Takaki, R. T. (1993). *A different mirror: A history of multicultural America*. Boston, MA: Little, Brown and Company.

A nonfiction book of history written by historian Ronald Takaki. This book covers several minority groups within the United States, surveying their unique histories and highlighting important points and events. One important contribution of this work is its emphasis on how minority group members themselves have perceived and understood their own history and experiences. Another important contribution of this work is its explanation of how the elite owners of capital in the United States have routinely used intergroup enmity as a way to keep labor under control.

Tatum, B. D. (2017). *Why are all the Black kids sitting together in the cafeteria?: And other conversations about race* (2nd ed.). New York, NY: Basic Books.

A nonfiction book written by a clinical psychologist, educator, and administrator who is well known for her writing and teaching about race. In this updated second edition (the first was published in 1997), Tatum reviews recent events in American racial history, covering the important ways in which American racial attitudes have changed (and not changed) in the years since the first edition. She covers important political and cultural events, including key policy changes and social movements (e.g., police shootings, Black Lives Matter protests). She then goes on to cover the phases of racial identity development for both Black and White people as well as how other American racial groups have been racialized and how that process has shaped their identities. Tatum covers a lot of ground with respect to the psychology of race and racism and finishes with a thoughtful consideration of why conversation on these topics matters and how individuals can find their own voices.

Treuer, D. (2012). *Rez Life: An Indian's journey through reservation life*. New York, NY: Atlantic Monthly Press.

A nonfiction book consisting of history, journalism, and memoir written by a novelist and writing professor at the University of Southern California. This book covers a variety of topics, most of which are misunderstood with respect to Native Americans, including but not limited to casinos, poverty, crime, daily reservation life, treaty rights, and language. Stories and evidence are used to illuminate and help the reader understand how policies and events have shaped the lives of contemporary Native Americans. The reader also gains a clearer picture of how and why non-Native Americans perceive and understand Native Americans in such limited and stereotyped ways.

Wilkerson, I. (2010). *The warmth of other suns: The epic story of America's great migration*. New York, NY: Random House.

A nonfiction book of narrative history written by the journalist Isabel Wilkerson. In it, Wilkerson makes the case convincingly that the migration of an estimated six million African Americans from the South to the North and West from roughly 1915 to 1970 was one of the most important internal migrations in American history. She tells the larger story through the life stories of three main protagonists, weaving their dramatic personal experiences into the larger narrative of how the great migration happened and how it has remained unrecognized for its importance to our history. She also helps us understand how racial discrimination in northern cities has led to the sustained inequality and injustice we see today.

Zinn, H. (1995). *A people's history of the United States: 1492 to present* (2nd ed.). New York, NY: HarperCollins.

This classic book of history was first published in 1980 by political scientist and historian Howard Zinn. The book was notable for its explicit focus on those who held less power, the people rather than the presidents and traditional leaders. In covering American history, Zinn focused on those who fought against the prevailing laws and policies of each historical era including those who resisted and opposed slavery, labor organizers, and anti-war protestors. Zinn was open in his attempt to subvert the traditional norms of academic history to that point, arguing that it is important for all people to better understand how power and injustice can be resisted.

REFERENCES

——

Adams, G., Tormala, T. T., & O'Brien, L. T. (2006). Effect of self-affirmation on the perception of racism. *Journal of Experimental Social Psychology, 42,* 616–626. doi:10.1037/e680122007-0001

Adams, M., Bell, L. A., Goodman, D. J., & Joshi, K. Y. (Eds). (2016). *Teaching for diversity and social justice* (3rd ed.). New York, NY: Routledge.

Adelman, L. (Producer). (2003). *Race: The power of an illusion.* [Television series]. San Francisco, CA: California Newsreel.

Ahluwalia, M. K., Ayala, S. I., Locke, A. F., Nadrich, T. (in press). Mitigating the "powder keg": The experiences of faculty of color teaching multicultural competence. *Teaching of Psychology.*

Ambrose, S. A., Bridges, M. W., DiPietro, M., Lovett, M. C., & Norman, M. K. (2010). *How learning works: Seven research-based principles for smart teaching.* San Francisco, CA: Jossey-Bass.

Anderson, C. (2016). *White rage: The unspoken truth of our racial divide.* New York, NY: Bloomsbury.

Angelo, T. A., & Cross, K. P. (1993). *Classroom assessment techniques: A handbook for college teachers.* San Francisco, CA: Jossey-Bass.

Apfelbaum, E. P., Norton, M. I., & Sommers, S. R. (2012). Racial color blindness. *Current Directions in Psychological Science, 21*(3), 205–209. doi:10.1177/0963721411434980

Apfelbaum, E. P., Sommers, S. R., & Norton, M. I. (2008). Seeing race and seeming racist? Evaluating strategic colorblindness in social interaction. *Journal of Personality and Social Psychology, 95*(4), 918–932. doi:10.1037/a0011990

Arao, B., & Clemens, K. (2013). From safe spaces to brave spaces: A new way to frame dialogue around diversity and social justice. In L. M. Landreman (Ed.), *The art of effective facilitation: Reflections from social justice educators* (pp. 135–150). Sterling, VA: Stylus.

Armstrong, M. J., & Wildman, S. J. (2013). Colorblindness is the new racism. In K. A. Case (Ed.), *Deconstructing privilege: Teaching and learning as allies in the classroom* (pp. 63–79). New York, NY: Routledge.

Astor, M. (2017, October 31). John Kelly pins Civil War on a "Lack of Ability to Compromise." *New York Times*. Retrieved from https://www.nytimes .com/2017/10/31/us/john-kelly-civil-war.html?_r=1

Avery, D. R., Richeson, J. A., Hebl, M. R., & Ambady, N. (2009). It does not have to be uncomfortable: The role of behavioral scripts in Black–White interracial interactions. *Journal of Applied Psychology, 94*(6), 1382–1393. doi:10.1037/a0016208

Babbitt, L. G., & Sommers, S. R. (2011). Framing matters. *Personality and Social Psychology Bulletin, 37*(9), 1233–1244. doi:10.1177/0146167211 410070

Bain, K. (2004). *What the best college teachers do.* Boston, MA: Harvard University Press.

Baker, K. J. (2016, February 23). *Academic waste.* Retrieved from https:// chroniclevitae.com/news/1301-academic-waste

Ball, C. E., & Loewe, D. M. (2017). *Bad ideas about writing.* Morgantown, WV: West Virginia University Libraries Digital Publishing Institute.

Banaji, M. R., & Greenwald, A. G. (2013). *Blindspot: Hidden biases of good people.* New York, NY: Delacorte.

Baptist, E. E. (2014). *The half has never been told: Slavery and the making of American capitalism.* New York, NY: Basic Books.

Barbezat, D. P., & Bush, M. (2014). *Contemplative practices in higher education.* San Francisco, CA: Jossey-Bass.

Bavishi, A., Madera, J. M., & Hebl, M. R. (2010). The effect of professor ethnicity and gender on student evaluations: Judged before met. *Journal of Diversity in Higher Education, 3*(4), 245–256. doi:10.1037 /a0020763

Biewen, J. (2017). Seeing white [Audio podcast]. *Scene on Radio Podcast.* Retrieved from http://podcast.cdsporch.org/seeing-white/

Binder, D. (2014). *DBR MTV Bias summary survey.* Retrieved from http:// d1fqdnmgwphrky.cloudfront.net/studies/000/000/001/DBR_MTV _Bias_Survey_Executive_Summary.pdf?1398858309

Biss, E. (2015, December 2). White debt. *New York Times.* Retrieved from https://www.nytimes.com/2015/12/06/magazine/white-debt .html?_r=0

Blackmon, D. A. (2008). *Slavery by another name: The re-enslavement of Black Americans from the Civil War to World War II.* New York, NY: Doubleday.

Boatright-Horowitz, S. L., & Soeung, S. (2009). Teaching White privilege to White students can mean saying good-bye to positive student evaluations. *American Psychologist, 64*(6), 574–575. doi:10.1037 /a0016593

Bowman, N. A. (2009). College diversity courses and cognitive development among students from privileged and marginalized groups. *Journal of Diversity in Higher Education, 2*(3), 182–194. doi:10.1037/a0016639

Boysen, G. A. (2017). Evidence-based answers to questions about trigger warnings for clinically-based distress: A review for teachers. *Scholarship of Teaching and Learning in Psychology, 3*(2), 163–177. doi:10.1037/stl 0000084

Boysen, G. A., Wells, A. M., & Dawson, K. J. (2016). Instructors' use of trigger warnings and behavior warnings in abnormal psychology. *Teaching of Psychology, 43*(4), 334–339. doi:10.1177/009862831666 2766

Brach, T. (n.d.). *How to meditate.* Retrieved from https://www.tarabrach .com/wp-content/uploads/pdf/HowToMeditateForPDF.pdf

Brady, S. T., Reeves, S. L., Garcia, J., Purdie-Vaughns, V., Cook, J. E., Taborsky-Barba, S., . . . Cohen, G. L. (2016). The psychology of the affirmed learner: Spontaneous self-affirmation in the face of stress. *Journal of Educational Psychology, 108*(3), 353–373. doi:10.1037/edu 0000091

Brookfield, S. D. (2015). *The skillful teacher: On technique, trust, and responsiveness in the classroom.* San Francisco, CA: Jossey-Bass.

Cabrera, N. L. (2017). White immunity: Working through some of the pedagogical pitfalls of "privilege." *Journal Committed to Social Change on Race and Ethnicity, 3*(1), 78–90.

Case, K. A. (Ed.). (2013). *Deconstructing privilege: Teaching and learning as allies in the classroom.* New York, NY: Routledge.

Case, K. A., & Cole, E. R. (2013). Deconstructing privilege when students resist. In K. A. Case (Ed.), *Deconstructing privilege: Teaching and learning as allies in the classroom.* New York, NY: Routledge.

Cavanagh, S. R. (2016). *The spark of learning: Energizing the college classroom with the science of emotion.* Morgantown, WV: West Virginia University Press.

Center for Research on Learning and Teaching. (2016). Overview of inclusive teaching at Michigan. Retrieved from http://crlt.umich.edu /overview-inclusive-teaching-michigan

Chappell, B. (2010, November 3). Bush says Kanye West's attack was low point of his presidency; West agrees. *NPR.* Retrieved from https://www .npr.org/sections/thetwo-way/2010/11/03/131052717/bush-says -kanye-west-s-attack-was-low-point-of-his-presidency

Cheryan, S., Plaut, V. C., Davies, P. G., & Steele, C. M. (2009). Ambient belonging: How stereotypical cues impact gender participation in computer science. *Journal of Personality and Social Psychology, 97*(6), 1045–1060. doi:10.1037/a0016239

Chick, N. L., Karis, T., & Kernahan, C. (2009). Learning from their own learning: How metacognitive and meta-affective reflections enhance learning in race-related courses. *International Journal for the Scholarship of Teaching and Learning, 3*(1). doi:10.20429/ijsotl.2009.030116

Cho, H. (2011). Lessons learned: Teaching the race concept in the college classroom. *Multicultural Perspectives, 13*(1), 36–41. doi:10.1080/15210 960.2011.548189

Cho, N. (2014, February 4). How I learned to feel undesirable [Blog post]. *NPR.* Retrieved from https://www.npr.org/sections/codeswitch /2014/02/04/271410342/how-i-learned-to-feel-undesirable

Cobb, J. (2017, November 1). John Kelly's bizarre mythology of the Civil War. *The New Yorker.* Retrieved from https://www.newyorker .com/news/news-desk/john-kellys-bizarre-mythology-of-the-civil -war

Cohen, G. L., & Sherman, D. K. (2014). The psychology of change: Self-affirmation and social psychological intervention. *Annual Review of Psychology, 65*(1), 333–371. doi:10.1146/annurev-psych-010213 -115137

Cohen, G. L., Steele, C. M., & Ross, L. D. (1999). The mentor's dilemma: Providing critical feedback across the racial divide. *Personality and Social Psychology Bulletin, 25*(10), 1302–1318. doi:10.1177/0146167299258011

Cottom, T. M. (2013, December 3). When students are treated like customers, racism and sexism win out. *Slate.* Retrieved from http://www.slate.com /articles/life/counter_narrative/2013/12/minneapolis_professor _shannon_gibney_reprimanded_for_talking_about_racism.html

Cottom, T. M. (2015, March 17). Starbucks wants to talk to you about race. But does it want to talk to you about racism? [Blog post]. Retrieved from https://medium.com/message/starbucks-wants-to-talk-to-you -about-race-but-does-it-want-to-talk-to-you-about-racism-63e13f03 3f5d

Crandall, C. S., Eidelman, S., Skitka, L. J., & Morgan, G. S. (2009). Status quo framing increases support for torture. *Social Influence, 4*(1), 1–10. doi:10.1080/15534510802124397

Crandall, C. S., & White, M. H. (2016, November 17). Donald Trump and the social psychology of prejudice [Blog post]. Retrieved from https:// undark.org/article/trump-social-psychology-prejudice-unleashed

Critcher, C. R., & Dunning, D. (2015). Self-affirmations provide a broader perspective on self-threat. *Personality and Social Psychology Bulletin, 41*(1), 3–18. doi:10.1177/0146167214554956

Crittle, C., & Maddox, K. B. (2017). Confronting bias through teaching. *Teaching of Psychology, 44*(2), 174–180. doi:10.1177/009862831769 2648

Crosby, J. R., King, M., & Savitsky, K. (2014). The minority spotlight effect. *Social Psychological and Personality Science, 5*(7), 743–750. doi:10.1177/1948550614527625

Cundiff, J. L., Zawadzki, M. J., Danube, C. L., & Shields, S. A. (2014). Using experiential learning to increase the recognition of everyday sexism as harmful: The WAGES intervention. *Journal of Social Issues, 70*(4), 703–721. doi:10.1111/josi.12087

Desmond-Harris, J. (2015, June 22). Stop waiting for racism to die out with old people. The Charleston shooting suspect is 21. *Vox.* Retrieved from https://www.vox.com/2015/6/22/8810539/racism-generational -american-views

DiAngelo, R. (2011). White fragility. *International Journal of Critical Pedagogy, 3*(3), 54–70.

Djikic, M., & Oatley, K. (2014). The art in fiction: From indirect communication to changes of the self. *Psychology of Aesthetics, Creativity, and the Arts, 8*(4), 498–505. doi:10.1037/a0037999

Djikic, M., Oatley, K., & Moldoveanu, M. C. (2013). Opening the closed mind: The effect of exposure to literature on the need for closure. *Creativity Research Journal, 25*(2), 149–154. doi:10.1080/10400419.20 13.783735

Dobbin, F., & Kalev, A. (2013). The origins and effects of corporate diversity programs. In Q. M. Roberson (Ed.), *The Oxford Handbook of Diversity and Work* (pp. 253–281). Oxford: Oxford University Press.

Evans, D. R., Boggero, I. A., & Segerstrom, S. C. (2016). The nature of self-regulatory fatigue and "Ego Depletion": Lessons from physical fatigue. *Personality and Social Psychology Review, 20*(4), 291–310. doi:10.1177/1088868315597841

Fallon, D. (2006). "Lucky to live in Maine": Examining student responses to diversity issues. *Teaching English in the Two-Year College, 33*(4), 410–420.

Flaherty, C. (2013, December 3). Taboo subject? *Inside Higher Ed.* Retrieved from https://www.insidehighered.com/news/2013/12/03/black -professors-essay-raises-questions-why-she-was-investigated-after -offending

Flaherty, C. (2015, May 14). Professor meets world. *Inside Higher Ed.* Retrieved from https://www.insidehighered.com/news/2015/05/14 /what-happens-when-scholars-discuss-potentially-controversial-ideas -outside-bubbles

Flaherty, C. (2016, May 18). Professor cleared and still out of a job. *Inside Higher Ed.* Retrieved from https://www.insidehighered.com/news /2016/05/18/professor-says-she-was-fired-over-well-intentioned-ill -received-class-discussion

Fredrickson, B. L. (2013). *Love 2.0: How our supreme emotion affects everything we feel, think, do, and become.* New York, NY: Hudson Street Press.

Fredrickson, B. L., Cohn, M. A., Coffey, K. A., Pek, J., & Finkel, S. M. (2008). Open hearts build lives: Positive emotions, induced through loving-kindness meditation, build consequential personal resources. *Journal of Personality and Social Psychology, 95*(5), 1045–1062. doi:10.1037/a0013262

Gallaher, C. A. (2011). *Rethinking the color line: Readings in race and ethnicity* (5th ed.). New York, NY: McGraw Hill Education.

Gannon, K. (2018, February 27). The case for inclusive teaching. *The Chronicle of Higher Education*. Retrieved from https://www.chronicle.com/article /The-Case-for-Inclusive/242636

Goff, P. A., Lloyd, T., Geller, A., Raphael, S., & Glaser, J. (2016, July). *The science of justice: Race, arrests, and police use of force*. Retrieved from Center for Policing Equity website: http://policingequity.org/wp -content/uploads/2016/07/CPE_SoJ_Race-Arrests-UoF_2016-07 -08-1130.pdf

Gonzalez, C. G. and Harris, A. P. (2012). Introduction. *Presumed incompetent: The intersections of race and class for women in academia.* Boulder, CO: University Press of Colorado.

Goodboy, A. K. (2011). Instructional dissent in the college classroom. *Communication Education, 60*(3), 296–313. doi:10.1080/03634523.2010 .537756

Hannah-Jones, N. (2014). Segregation now. *ProPublica.* Retrieved from https://www.propublica.org/article/segregation-now-the-resegregation -of-americas-schools/#james

Hetter, K. (2015, May 13). Fury over Boston University professor's tweets. *CNN.* Retrieved from http://www.cnn.com/2015/05/13/living/feat -boston-university-saida-grundy-race-tweets/index.html

Hölzel, B. K., Lazar, S. W., Gard, T., Schuman-Olivier, Z., Vago, D. R., & Ott, U. (2011). How does mindfulness meditation work? Proposing mechanisms of action from a conceptual and neural perspective. *Perspectives on Psychological Science, 6*(6), 537–559. doi:10.1177/1745691611419671

Howard, J. R. (2015). *Discussion in the college classroom: Getting your students engaged and participating in person and online.* San Francisco, CA: Jossey-Bass.

Isenberg, N. (2016). *White trash: The 400-year untold history of class in America.* New York, NY: Viking.

Jaschik, S. (2015, August 24). Saida Grundy, moving forward. *Inside Higher Ed.* Retrieved from https://www.insidehighered.com/news/2015/08 /24/saida-grundy-discusses-controversy-over-her-comments-twitter -her-career-race-and

Jaschik, S. (2016, March 21). Professor cleared to teach after furor over race. *Inside Higher Ed.* Retrieved from https://www.insidehighered.com /news/2016/03/21/u-kansas-professor-cleared-teach-after-controversy -over-discussion-race

Jones, J. M. (1996). *Prejudice and racism.* New York, NY: McGraw-Hill.

Jones, R. P., Cox, D., Cooper, B., & Lienesch, R. (2015). *Anxiety, nostalgia, and mistrust: Findings from the 2015 American Values Survey.* Retrieved from PRRI website: https://www.prri.org/research/survey-anxiety-nostalgia-and-mistrust-findings-from-the-2015-american-values-survey

Jost, J. T. (2011). System justification theory as compliment, complement, and corrective to theories of social identification and social dominance. In D. Dunning (Ed.), *Frontiers of social psychology. Social motivation* (pp. 223–263). New York, NY: Psychology Press.

Kantrowitz, M. (2011, September 2). *The Distribution of grants and scholarships by race. FinAid.org.* Retrieved from http://www.finaid.org/scholarships/20110902racescholarships.pdf

Kendi, I. (2016). *Stamped from the beginning: The definitive history of racist ideas in America.* New York, NY: Nation Books.

Kernahan, C., & Davis, T. (2007). Changing perspective: How learning about racism influences student awareness and emotion. *Teaching of Psychology, 34*(1), 49–52. doi:10.1207/s15328023top3401_12

Kernahan, C., & Davis, T. (2010). What are the long-term effects of learning about racism? *Teaching of Psychology, 37*(1), 41–45. doi:10.1080/00986280903425748

Kernahan, C., Zheng, W., & Davis, T. (2014). A sense of belonging: How student feelings correlate with learning about race. *International Journal for the Scholarship of Teaching and Learning, 8*(2). doi:10.20429/ijsotl.2014.080204

Kinzel, L. (2012, November 13). *ASK LESLEY: How do I stop accidentally offending people all the time?* Retrieved from https://www.xojane.com/issues/ask-lesley-how-do-i-stop-accidentally-offending-people-all-the-time

Kumanyika, C. (2015, June 24). Dispatch from Charleston: The cost of White comfort [Blog post]. *NPR.* Retrieved from https://www.npr.org/sections/codeswitch/2015/06/24/417108714/dispatch-from-charleston-the-cost-of-white-comfort

Lambert, N. M., Stillman, T. F., Hicks, J. A., Kamble, S., Baumeister, R. F., & Fincham, F. D. (2013). To belong is to matter. *Personality and Social Psychology Bulletin, 39*(11), 1418–1427. doi:10.1177/0146167213499186

Lang, J. M. (2016). *Small teaching: Everyday lessons from the science of learning.* San Francisco, CA: Jossey-Bass.

Lee, E. (2015). *The making of Asian America: A history.* New York, NY: Simon and Schuster.

Legault, L., Gutsell, J. N., & Inzlicht, M. (2011). Ironic effects of antiprejudice messages: How motivational interventions can reduce (but also increase) prejudice. *Psychological Science, 22*(12), 1472–1477.

Lensmire, T., McManimon, S., Tierney, J. D., Lee-Nichols, M., Casey, Z., Lensmire, A., & Davis, B. (2013). McIntosh as synecdoche: How teacher education's focus on White privilege undermines antiracism. *Harvard Educational Review, 83*(3), 410–431. doi:10.17763/haer.83.3 .35054h14l8230574

Lewandowsky, S., Ecker, U. K., Seifert, C. M., Schwarz, N., & Cook, J. (2012). Misinformation and its correction. *Psychological Science in the Public Interest, 13*(3), 106–131. doi:10.1177/1529100612451018

Lindquist, E. (2017, October 28). UW-EC English class teaches lessons on Whiteness. *Leader-Telegram*. Retrieved from http://www.leadertelegram .com/News/Front-Page/2017/10/28/Whites-on-white.html

Loewen, J. W. (2018). *Lies my teacher told me: Everything your American history textbook got wrong* (2nd ed.). New York, NY: The New Press.

MacNell, L., Driscoll, A., & Hunt, A. N. (2015). What's in a name: Exposing gender bias in student ratings of teaching. *Innovative Higher Education, 40*(4), 291–303. doi:10.1007/s10755-014-9313-4

McElwee, S. (2015, March 24). The hidden racism of young White Americans. *PBS*. Retrieved from https://www.pbs.org/newshour/nation /americas-racism-problem-far-complicated-think

McFarland, J., Hussar, B., Wang, X., Zhang, J., Wang, K., Rathbun, A., Barmer, A., Forrest Cataldi, E., and Bullock Mann, F. (2018). *The condition of education 2018* (NCES 2018–144). U.S. Department of Education. Washington, DC: National Center for Education Statistics. Retrieved from https://nces.ed.gov/pubsearch/pubsinfo.asp?pubid= 2018144

McGinley, J. J., & Jones, B. D. (2014). A brief instructional intervention to increase students' motivation on the first day of class. *Teaching of Psychology, 41*(2), 158–162. doi:10.1177/0098628314530350

McIntosh, P. (1988). *White privilege and male privilege: A personal account of coming to see correspondence through work in women's studies* (Working Paper 189). Wellesley, MA: Wellesley Center for Research on Women.

Mekawi, Y., & Bresin, K. (2015). Is the evidence from racial bias shooting task studies a smoking gun? Results from a meta-analysis. *Journal of Experimental Social Psychology, 61,* 120–130. doi:10.1016/j.jesp.2015 .08.002

Meyer, J. H., & Land, R. (2005). Threshold concepts and troublesome knowledge (2): Epistemological considerations and a conceptual framework for teaching and learning. *Higher Education, 49*(3), 373–388. doi:10.1007/s10734-004-6779-5

Moss-Racusin, C. A., Toorn, J. V., Dovidio, J. F., Brescoll, V. L., Graham,

M. J., & Handelsman, J. (2014). Scientific diversity interventions. *Science, 343*(6171), 615–616. doi:10.1126/science.1245936

National Center against Censorship. (2015, December). What's all this about trigger warnings? Retrieved from http://ncac.org/wp-content /uploads/2015/11/NCAC-TriggerWarningReport.pdf

Newport, F. (2017, January 18). Americans' satisfaction steady or up, except on race matters. *Gallup.* Retrieved from http://news.gallup .com/poll/202568/americans-satisfaction-steady-except-race-matters .aspx?version=print

Norton, M. I., & Sommers, S. R. (2011). Whites see racism as a zero-sum game that they are now losing. *Perspectives on Psychological Science, 6,* 215–218. doi:10.1037/e634112013-24

Nosek, B. A., Smyth, F. L., Hansen, J. J., Devos, T., Lindner, N. M., Ranganath, K. A., . . . Banaji, M. R. (2007). Pervasiveness and correlates of implicit attitudes and stereotypes. *European Review of Social Psychology, 18*(1), 36–88. doi:10.1080/10463280701489053

Nott, J. C., & Gliddon, G. R. (1854). *Types of mankind: Or, ethnological researches based upon the ancient monuments, paintings, sculptures, and crania of races, and upon their natural, geographical, philological and biblical history, illustrated by selections from the inedited papers of Samuel George Morton and by additional contributions from L. Agassiz, W. Usher, and H.S. Patterson.* Philadelphia, PA: J.B. Lippincott, Grambo & Co.

NPR. (2017, November). *Discrimination in America: Experiences and views of White Americans.* Retrieved from https://www.npr.org/documents /2017/oct/discrimination-whites-final.pdf

NPR. (2017). *You, me and them: Experiencing discrimination in America.* Retrieved from https://www.npr.org/series/559149737/you-me-and -them-experiencing-discrimination-in-america

Omi, M., & Winant, H. (2015). *Racial formation in the United States* (3rd ed.). New York, NY: Routledge.

Painter, N. I. (2010). *The history of White people.* New York, NY: W.W. Norton and Company.

Parrott, H. M., & Cherry, E. (2011). Using structured reading groups to facilitate deep learning. *Teaching Sociology, 39*(4), 354–370. doi:10.1177/0092055x11418687

Pasque, P. A., Chesler, M. A., Charbeneau, J., & Carlson, C. (2013). Pedagogical approaches to student racial conflict in the classroom. *Journal of Diversity in Higher Education, 6*(1), 1–16. doi:10.1037 /a0031695

Patrick, S., & Connolly, C. M. (2013). The privilege project: A narrative approach for teaching social justice and multicultural awareness. *Journal of Systemic Therapies, 32*(1), 70–86. doi:10.1521/jsyt.2013 .32.1.70

Pauker, K., Apfelbaum, E. P., & Spitzer, B. (2015). When societal norms and social identity collide. *Social Psychological and Personality Science, 6*(8), 887–895. doi:10.1177/1948550615598379

Pew Research Center. (2010, January 11). *Blacks upbeat about black progress, prospects.* Retrieved from http://www.pewsocialtrends.org/2010/01/12 /blacks-upbeat-about-black-progress-prospects

Pew Research Center. (2013, August 22). *King's dream remains an elusive goal; Many Americans see racial disparities.* Retrieved from http://www .pewsocialtrends.org/2013/08/22/kings-dream-remains-an-elusive-goal -many-americans-see-racial-disparities

Pew Research Center. (2015, March 19). *Comparing millennials to other gen- erations.* Retrieved from http://www.pewsocialtrends.org/2015/03/19 /comparing-millennials-to-other-generations

Pew Research Center. (2016, June 27). *On views of race and inequality, Blacks and Whites are worlds apart.* Retrieved from http://www.pewsocialtrends .org/2016/06/27/on-views-of-race-and-inequality-blacks-and-whites -are-worlds-apart

Pew Research Center. (2017, October 5). *Partisan divides over political values widen.* Retrieved from http://www.people-press.org/2017/10/05/1 -partisan-divides-over-political-values-widen

Phillips, L. T., & Lowery, B. S. (2015). The hard-knock life? Whites claim hardships in response to racial inequity. *Journal of Experimental Social Psychology, 61,* 12–18. doi:10.1016/j.jesp.2015.06.008

Plaut, V. C., Garnett, F. G., Buffardi, L. E., & Sanchez-Burks, J. (2011). "What about me?" Perceptions of exclusion and Whites' reactions to multiculturalism. *Journal of Personality and Social Psychology, 101*(2), 337–353. doi:10.1037/a0022832

Reséndez, A. (2016). *The other slavery: The uncovered story of Indian enslavement in America.* New York, NY: Houghton Mifflin.

Rogers, D. T. (2015). Further validation of the learning alliance inventory. *Teaching of Psychology, 42*(1), 19–25. doi:10.1177/0098628314562673

Rosette, A. S., & Tost, L. P. (2013). Perceiving social inequity. *Psychological Science, 24*(8), 1420–1427. doi:10.1177/0956797612473608

Sandstrom, G. M., & Dunn, E. W. (2014a). Is efficiency overrated?: Minimal social interactions lead to belonging and positive affect. *Social Psychological and Personality Science, 5*(4), 437–442. doi:10.1037 /e578192014-875

Sandstrom, G. M., & Dunn, E. W. (2014b). Social interactions and well- being. *Personality and Social Psychology Bulletin, 40*(7), 910–922. doi:10.1177/0146167214529799

Sandstrom, G. M., & Rawn, C. D. (2015). Embrace chattering students. *Teaching of Psychology, 42*(3), 227–233. doi:10.1177/009862831558 7620

Schumann, K., & Dweck, C. S. (2014). Who accepts responsibility for their transgressions? *Personality and Social Psychology Bulletin, 40*(12), 1598–1610. doi:10.1177/0146167214552789

Seidel, S. B., & Tanner, K. D. (2013). "What if students revolt?"— considering student resistance: Origins, options, and opportunities for investigation. *Cell Biology Education, 12*(4), 586–595. doi:10.1187/cbe -13-09-0190

Shih, D. (2015, January 23). White happened to you [Blog post]. Retrieved from http://professorshih.blogspot.com/2015/01/white-happened-to -you.html

Shih, D. (2015, February 27). White supremacy can make you poor [Blog post]. Retrieved from http://professorshih.blogspot.com/2015/02 /white-supremacy-can-make-you-poor.html

Shnabel, N., Purdie-Vaughns, V., Cook, J. E., Garcia, J., & Cohen, G. L. (2013). Demystifying values-affirmation interventions. *Personality and Social Psychology Bulletin, 39*(5), 663–676. doi:10.1177/014616721 3480816

Sidanius, J., Levin, S., Van Laar, C., & Sears, D. O. (2008). *The diversity challenge: Social identity and intergroup relations on the college campus.* New York, NY: Russell Sage Foundation.

Smedley, A. (2007). *The history of the idea of race . . . And why it matters.* Paper presented at the Race, Human Variation, and Disease: Consensus and Frontiers Conference sponsored by the American Anthropological Association, Warrenton, VA.

Smith, W. L., & Crowley, R. M. (2015). Pushback and possibility: Using a threshold concept of race in social studies teacher education. *The Journal of Social Studies Research, 39*(1), 17–28. doi:10.1016/j.jssr.2014.05.004

Southern Poverty Law Center. (2016, December 16). Update: 1,094 bias-related incidents in the month following the election. Retrieved from https://www.splcenter.org/hatewatch/2016/12/16/update-1094-bias -related-incidents-month-following-election

Stachowiak, B. (2017, April 6). Racial identity in the classroom [Audio podcast]. *Teaching in Higher Ed Podcast.* Retrieved from http:// teachinginhighered.com/podcast/racial-identity-classroom/

Starbucks. (2018, May 29). The third place: Our commitment, renewed. Retrieved from https://starbuckschannel.com/thethirdplace/

Stephens, N. M., Townsend, S. S., Hamedani, M. G., Destin, M., & Manzo, V. (2015). A difference-education intervention equips first-generation college students to thrive in the face of stressful college situations. *Psychological Science, 26*(10), 1556–1566. doi:10.1177/0956797615593501

Stevens, D. D., & Levi, A. J. (2012). *Introduction to rubrics* (2nd ed.). Sterling, VA: Stylus.

Stevens, F. G., Plaut, V. C., & Sanchez-Burks, J. (2008). Unlocking the benefits of diversity. *The Journal of Applied Behavioral Science, 44*(1), 116–133. doi:10.1177/0021886308314460

Sturmey P., Dalfen, S., & Fienup, D. M. (2015). Inter-teaching: A systematic review. *European Journal of Behavior Analysis, 16*(1), 121–130. doi:10.10 80/15021149.2015.1069655

Sue, D. W. (2015). *Race talk and the conspiracy of silence: Understanding and facilitating difficult dialogues on race*. Hoboken, NJ: Wiley.

Sue, D. W., Rivera, D. P., Watkins, N. L., Kim, R. H., Kim, S., & Williams, C. D. (2011). Racial dialogues: Challenges faculty of color face in the classroom. *Cultural Diversity and Ethnic Minority Psychology, 17*(3), 331–340. doi:10.1037/a0024190

Takaki, R. T. (1993). *A different mirror: A history of multicultural America*. Boston, MA: Little, Brown and Company.

Tatum, B. D. (1992). Talking about race, learning about racism: The application of racial identity development theory in the classroom. *Harvard Educational Review, 62*(1), 1–24. doi:10.4135/9781446220986 .n31

Tatum, B. D. (1994). Teaching White students about racism: The search for White allies and the restoration of hope. *Teachers College Record, 95*(4), 462–476.

Tatum, B. D. (2017). *Why are all the Black kids sitting together in the cafeteria?: And other conversations about race* (2nd ed.). New York, NY: Basic Books.

Tavris, C., & Aronson, E. (2015). *Mistakes were made (but not by me): Why we justify foolish beliefs, bad decisions, and hurtful acts*. New York, NY: Houghton Mifflin Harcourt.

Toosi, N. R., Babbitt, L. G., Ambady, N., & Sommers, S. R. (2012). Dyadic interracial interactions: A meta-analysis. *Psychological Bulletin, 138*(1), 1–27. doi:10.1037/e527772014-146

Trawalter, S., & Richeson, J. A. (2008). Let's talk about race, baby! When Whites' and Blacks' interracial contact experiences diverge. *Journal of Experimental Social Psychology, 44*(4), 1214–1217. doi:10.1016/j.jesp .2008.03.013

Treuer, D. (2012). *Rez Life: An Indian's journey through reservation life*. New York, NY: Atlantic Monthly Press.

Tropp, L., & Page-Gould, E. (2015). Contact between groups. In Mikulincer, M., Shaver, P. R., Dovidio, J. F., & Simpson, J. A. (Eds), *APA handbook of personality and social psychology, Volume 2: Group processes* (pp. 535–560). Washington, DC: American Psychological Association.

Vittrup, B. (2018). Color blind or color conscious? White American mothers' approaches to racial socialization. *Journal of Family Issues, 39*(3), 668–692. https://doi.org/10.1177/0192513X16676858

Wade, L. M. (2015, June 23). Millennials are no less racist than

Generation X [Blog post]. *Sociological Images*. Retrieved from https://thesocietypages.org/socimages/2015/06/23/millennials-are-no-less-racist-than-generation-x-hardly-different-from-boomers

Walton, G. M., & Cohen, G. L. (2011). A brief social-belonging intervention improves academic and health outcomes of minority students. *Science, 331*(6023), 1447–1451. doi:10.1126/science.1198364

Waring, C. D. L., & Bordoloi, S. D. (2012). "Hopping on the tips of a trident": Two graduate students of color reflect on teaching critical content at predominantly White institutions. *Feminist Teacher, 22*(2), 108. doi:10.5406/femteacher.22.2.0108

Washington Post. (2017). *Police shootings 2017 database*. Retrieved December 15, 2017, from https://www.washingtonpost.com/graphics/national/police-shootings-2017/

Wilkerson, I. (2010). *The warmth of other suns: The epic story of America's great migration*. New York, NY: Random House.

Williams, K., & Gibney, S. (2014, October 31). Surviving blackademia. *Inside Higher Ed*. Retrieved from https://www.insidehighered.com/advice/2014/10/31/tips-surviving-and-thriving-black-female-professor-essay

Wilson, J. H., & Ryan, R. G. (2013). Professor–student rapport scale. *Teaching of Psychology, 40*(2), 130–133. doi:10.1177/0098628312475033

Wilson, T. D. (2011). *Redirect: The surprising new science of psychological change*. New York, NY: Little, Brown and Company.

Winkler, E. N. (2018). Racism as a threshold concept: Examining learning in a "diversity requirement" course. *Race Ethnicity and Education, 21*(6), 1–19. doi:10.1080/13613324.2017.1294564

Wise, T. (2011). *White like me: Reflections on race from a privileged son*. Berkeley, CA: Soft Skull Press.

Wise, T., & Case, K. A. (2013). Pedagogy for the privileged. In K. A. Case (Ed.), *Deconstructing privilege: Teaching and learning as allies in the classroom*. New York, NY: Routledge.

WPR. (2015, March 19). *Starbucks launches #RaceTogether campaign*. Retrieved from https://www.wpr.org/starbucks-launches-racetogether-campaign

Yeager, D. S., Henderson, M. D., Paunesku, D., Walton, G. M., D'Mello, S., Spitzer, B. J., & Duckworth, A. L. (2014). Boring but important: A self-transcendent purpose for learning fosters academic self-regulation. *Journal of Personality and Social Psychology, 107*(4), 559–580. doi:10.1037/a0037637

Yeager, D. S., Purdie-Vaughns, V., Garcia, J., Apfel, N., Brzustoski, P., Master, A., . . . Cohen, G. L. (2014). Breaking the cycle of mistrust: Wise interventions to provide critical feedback across the racial divide. *Journal of Experimental Psychology: General, 143*(2), 804–824. doi:10.1037/a0033906

Yeager, D. S., Walton, G. M., Brady, S. T., Akcinar, E. N., Paunesku, D., Keane, L., . . . Dweck, C. S. (2016). Teaching a lay theory before college narrows achievement gaps at scale. *PNAS, 113*(24), 3341–3348. doi:10.1073/pnas.1524360113

Zheng, L. (2016, May 15). Why your brave space sucks. Retrieved from https://www.stanforddaily.com/2016/05/15/why-your-brave-space -sucks

Zinn, H. (1995). *A people's history of the United States: 1492 to present* (2nd ed.). New York, NY: HarperCollins.

INDEX
